UNDERGROUND MAN

Underground Man

EDWARD F. ABOOD

Chandler & Sharp Publishers, Inc.

San Francisco

The author and publisher very gratefully acknowledge permission to reprint in revised form materials from the following publications:

Chapter 3 (Hermann Hesse: *Steppenwolf*) appeared originally (in modified form) as "Jung's Concept of Individuation in Hesse's *Steppenwolf*" in *Southern Humanities Review*, Winter 1968, pp. 1-13. Chapter 6 (Jean Genet: *Our Lady of the Flowers*) appeared in an earlier version as "Genet: An Underground Man" in *Psychological Perspectives*, Vol. 2, No. 2 (Fall 1971).

Abood, Edward F
    Underground man.

    1.   Literature, Modern—20th century—History and
criticism. 2.   Alienation (Social psychology) in
literature.   I.   Title.
PN771.A2   809.3'3   72-97331
ISBN 0-88316-048-X

Book designed by Joseph M. Roter

CONTENTS

UNDERGROUND MAN

INTRODUCTION

Today, the term *underground* evokes a kaleidoscope of images, including revolution, communes, love-ins, avant-garde newspapers, and drugs. But the current associations of this word derive from an older and more fundamental meaning of the term. For this definition we must go back to Dostoevsky's *Notes from Underground*.

It is now over a hundred years since Dostoevsky wrote his prophetic work. Yet while he has become a classic literary figure, Dostoevsky's immortal neurotic, Underground Man,[1] speaks to more kindred souls today than he did in 1864. The strident protest which he first raised against the established order has been echoed by a multitude of famous descendants: Céline's Bardamu, adrift in a postwar wasteland; Hemingway's Jake Barnes, sipping absinthe to sweeten the bitter pill of nada; Hesse's Steppenwolf, prowling the hostile streets of the bourgeoisie to escape the razor waiting for him at home; Kafka's crepuscular K.'s, stumbling down corridors that lead nowhere; Sartre's lonely Existentialist, determined to create himself in a wilderness abandoned by God; Camus' Absurd Man, finding his only satisfaction in the knowledge that the universe does not make sense; Ellison's Invisible Man, struggling to make himself visible; Koestler's Rubashov, betrayed by the Communist gods of his own creation; Genet's Jean, consummating an unsanctioned marriage with cutthroats and male prostitutes.

Despite their often radical differences, these protagonists constitute a single type, which we may designate as *underground man*. Underground man is generally a rebel against the prevailing norms of the society he lives

---

[1] Dostoevsky's Underground Man will be capitalized throughout the book. All references to underground man in general will be in lower case.

1

in and the great forces that perpetuate them: government, the military, business, labor, the mass media, the classroom, the pulpit—institutional powers of any sort. He may even extend his indictment to include not only society, but Nature, Being or God as well. His antipathy may become active revolt, or it may turn in upon itself, reducing him to despair and a longing for death. But whatever action he takes (if he is capable of action), it is always essentially personal; even when he joins a group, his commitment is subjective, and he is thus ultimately isolated. Moreover, his characteristic attitude is negation; if he does develop a positive philosophy of his own, it begins with, and is conditioned by, a denial of other codes of conduct, particularly the values by which the majority of his contemporaries live. Consequently, he lives in a constant state of tension and anxiety, aggravated by what is perhaps his most distinguishing quality—a keen, often morbid, sensibility.

While many of these qualities are centuries old, their peculiar synthesis into underground man is a strictly modern development. He is essentially a reaction to forces of the past century, the descriptions of which have been repeated so often that they are now truisms on the lips of school-boys: the climax and denouement of imperialism in a series of global wars; the emergence of modern Leviathans—the Fascist, the Communist, the Welfare states; the violent acceleration of industrialization, with its virtual obliteration of rural life, its transformation of the cities into overcrowded infernos and the countryside into monotonous suburbia, its dreary cycles of prosperity and bust; the triumph of organization, the dilution of culture, the refinement of the Establishment, the anaesthetization of mass man, the dehumanization of art, the despiritualization of religion, and so on.

Significantly, *Notes from Underground* was written five years after the publication of Darwin's *Origin of Species*. In Darwin's repudiation of Biblical authority (already severely weakened), responsive underground man suddenly saw the ordered universe of his fathers give way to the chaos of the jungle. He began to ask disturbing questions which, in days gone by, would have landed him in Bedlam or brought down on him the *auto-da-fé*: If what we call reason and will are only "characteristics" favoring the "survival" of the highest "species," then what meaning shall we give to such traditional abstractions as truth, beauty, justice and honor? If man is simply an organism responding to stimuli, then in what way is he free? And what sort of moral responsibility are we to attribute to a creature that differs only quantitatively from the apes?

Science did not content itself with undermining the Christian view of man. In the century since the publication of *Notes from Underground,* it has even rejected many of its own former "certitudes." The "laws" of nature are now "probabilities"; absolute space is only a working hypothesis or a pragmatic tool; phenomena are discontinuous; the atom is simply a convenient metaphor to describe an unknown entity called matter, which is really only another form of energy. Paradoxically, what began as the most rational tool known to man has driven men to the extreme position of philosophical irrationalism, causing Albert Camus, in *The Myth of Sisyphus,* to conclude:

> With the exception of professional rationalists, today people despair of true knowledge. If the only significant history of human thought were to be written, it would have to be the history of its successive regrets and its impotence.

Various philosophers of the nineteenth and twentieth centuries—the Transcendentalists, the Utilitarians, the Marxists, the Evolutionists, the Positivists, the Whiteheadians—have cheerfully attempted to accommodate science and humanism. But underground man, of a more saturnine bent, sees little cause for rejoicing in the scientific view of man. He cannot reconcile it with his innermost yearning for the spirituality and metaphysical certainty of bygone ages, seeing in the materialist's conception of progress the realization of only one of man's potentialities while the others languish in neglect. At the same time, he cannot deny the authority of science—it is all around him, in the food he eats, the clothes he wears, and the apartment building he lives in. Moreover, since he has grown up in an age dominated by science, he has osmotically assimilated many of its premises, even though he knows that they lead not to the ultimate certainty he longs for, but to logical absurdity. Thus, though his senses confirm the scientific conception of reality, his very being rebels against it.

But there is one important constituent of underground man's makeup that antedates Darwin, having its origin in early nineteenth-century Romanticism. This is his heightened sense of the personal. He is always keenly conscious of his unique identity—whether to create his own values, like the Existentialists; to make peace with the external world contingent on reconciliation with the self, like Steppenwolf; or to find reality in his own dreams, like Genet's solipsistic Jean. He spends long lonely hours analyzing himself and his equivocal relation to the Other. Echoing Kierkegaard's rebellious cry, "The crowd is an untruth," he resists popular fads; and though he usually has a university education, he tends to view the world with the rough novelty and originality of the autodidact.

However, while the Romantic hero experienced joy in himself, the self to underground man is often his chief source of agony. Wordsworth obtained fulfillment by replenishing the self from Nature; Shelley arrived at beatitude by projecting it on Plato's world of pure form; Byron achieved apotheosis by heroically sacrificing it in "wars of liberation." Sophisticated underground man, on the other hand, would view these poets as innocents before the slaughter. For him there is no nature, only smog-ridden cities; there is no God, or if there is, underground man is not on good terms with Him; and though there are many wars, they are not noble, but dirty. Because the Romantic's sensibility was cushioned with these and other props, he could afford to indulge himself in "solitude," like one who goes to church in order to hear Bach played on the organ. But underground man does not choose his isolation—it is his burden and his lot. He needs no Ionesco to remind him that, "Cut off from his religious, metaphysical and transcendental roots, man is lost; all his actions become senseless, absurd, useless."

Underground man may not necessarily know more than the Romantic (though he is usually an intellectual); but what he does know is more relevant to his times. The Romantic of Wordsworth's day simply turned his back on urban society and the demoralizing effects of the Industrial Revolution; or if he did view them, it was usually at a comfortable distance. Nor did he evince much interest in science, politics or economics, even though they were transforming the world before his very eyes. Underground man, on the other hand, is only too aware of them. Even if he wanted to escape these forces he could not, because modern civilization is encroaching on him from all sides (Wordsworth's line, "The world is too much with us," is obviously more applicable to underground man than to Wordsworth). Hence underground man sees the world with the eyes of the realist; and with the world as it is, his lucidity is his torment.

Finally, he lacks the confidence and pride of the Romantic, or if on occasion he acquires them, it is only by means of a painful inner struggle. If he is not actually impotent and passive, like his contemporary, the Naturalistic hero, he feels his inadequacy nonetheless. Unlike Byron's Cain, or Shelley's Prometheus, he hesitates before he throws down the gauntlet to society and the gods, because revolt for him is not a style of living, it is a necessity. On those rare occasions when he actually does triumph over his environment, as in the fiction of Sartre, Hesse and Malraux, his victory is an uncertain one—he must continually reassure himself of it. And in those more frequent instances when he is defeated (as is invariably the case in Kafka's works), he succumbs not only to antagonists outside of himself but to crippling forces within his own psyche. The objective menace of the world becomes internalized, turning into guilt and anxiety, reducing him to a chronic state of malaise and debilitation. Doomed from the start, underground man at this extreme would scarcely be distinguishable from the unlucky protagonist of Naturalistic fiction were it not for his relentless consciousness of what is happening to him.

Thus isolated, uncommitted, having rejected traditional or current values without having substituted new ones for them, burdened with a consciousness that spares nothing, not even himself, underground man is a malcontent living in a continual state of anxiety and doubt. It goes without saying that the nameless narrator in *Notes from Underground* is the perfect embodiment of the type. He reappears, in modified form, in innumerable contemporary novels. But he is most conspicuous—despite his often radical permutations—in Kafka's *The Castle* (1926), Hesse's *Steppenwolf* (1927), Sartre's *Nausea* (1937), Camus' *The Fall* (1956), Genet's *Our Lady of the Flowers* (1943), Malraux's *Man's Fate* (1934), and Koestler's *Darkness at Noon* (1941).

These seven novels, together with *Notes from Underground,* constitute a kind of compendium of modern culture from 1864 to 1956. They are written by men who are not only acute observers but also original and, generally, profound philosophers. With the exception of Genet, all are also intellectuals. There is scarcely a political, scientific, psychological or philosophical theory of major importance in the past century that is not subsumed, either directly or indirectly, in their works. Their writings, in addition, are responsive to significant historical events, such as the two world wars and the rise of Communism.

Dostoevsky portrays underground man in czarist Russia anticipating the rise of Bolshevism; Koestler depicts his reactions to Bolshevism as an established fact in Russia three-quarters of a century later. Hesse places him in chaotic Germany after World War I. Sartre uses him to satirize the complacent French (and by implication European) bourgeoisie just before the shock of World War II; Camus' underground man resumes that satire after the War. Genet demonstrates, through his indifference to that war, that his underworld castoffs are the result of France's social, rather than political, maladies. Malraux not only follows the desperate European underground man to the Far East, but he also introduces the Oriental underground man, created by Europe's transformation of the Orient and abetted by his European counterpart in the role of criminal or revolutionist. Kafka portrays underground man in an ostensibly timeless world, but the Alpine village of *The Castle* is assimilated by what is unmistakably a modern, possibly totalitarian, bureaucracy.

Finally, underlying the social iconoclasm of these protagonists is their metaphysical discontent. Their fundamental lack is commitment to an absolute that justifies and gives meaning to their lives. In the centuries preceding the advent of underground man, religion provided that absolute. But underground man has either rejected God outright, or feels himself so alienated from Him that He has ceased to be a positive force in underground man's life. He must therefore either rediscover God or find some equivalent for Him.

The most hopeless character in this respect, and therefore the most unequivocally underground, is Dostoevsky's Underground Man. The author never tells us why or how he became an atheist. We can only surmise that he, like other Russian intellectuals (including the young Dostoevsky), was temporarily enamored of the secular rationalism popular in Western Europe at the time. According to this thinking, God was superfluous because, given human reason and perfectibility, man could build his own paradise here on earth. But skeptical Underground Man, like Dostoevsky himself, comes to doubt that man is either rational or perfectible or that there can ever be ultimate happiness which is not rooted in that very spirituality which these utopian philosophies exclude. Unlike Dostoevsky, though, Underground Man is incapable of or unwilling to return to his initial faith (again, Dostoevsky never tells us why). In other words, Underground Man rationally refutes a doctrine predicated on reason but lacks the faith that can take him beyond reason. Dostoevsky, then, introduces us to the spiritual limbo in which subsequent underground men will find themselves. But whereas each of them makes an attempt to move out of it, Dostoevsky's Underground Man, who despairs from the outset, is permanently fixed in it.

Like Dostoevsky, Kafka believes in God: God, the metaphysical extension of his natural father, is too rooted in Kafka's complex psyche to be denied. But if the Scriptures for Dostoevsky offer redemption, for Kafka they underscore man's fall from grace. Instead of drawing support from them, he experiences primarily guilt, anxiety and alienation. Thus despite his faith, Kafka is essentially an underground man. For though he never quite relinquishes hope that he will experience a happy union with God, his quest, like that of K. in *The Castle,* ends in frustration.

Hesse's God, on the other hand, is more accessible. He inheres in the world. Hence man can realize a cosmic order not through renunciation or asceticism, but through maximum knowledge and experience of this world. Moreover, Hesse postulates a practical "way" to God. More adaptable than either Christianity or Judaism to the dynamic pluralism of modern times, it is a unique synthesis of Zen-Taoism, on the one hand, and Jungian psychotherapy on the other. Although at the conclusion of *Steppenwolf* the hero is still floundering on the fringes of underground, he has caught glimpses of a goal and a method of achieving it. He is therefore one of the more "successful" underground men.

For Dostoevsky, Kafka and Hesse (all reared in the nineteenth century), the universe is governed by God, and man's reunion with God is always a metaphysical possibility. The more recent generation of writers—Sartre, Camus and Genet—see man as an isolated, gratuitous phenomenon and the universe as ultimately incomprehensible and absurd. God's revelation is the ultimate goal of the first group of underground writers; His categorical absence is the starting point for the second. Alienation for the latter becomes a positive individualism; the absence of an ultimate basis for knowledge is the spur to create a strictly human scheme of values.

Sartre and Dostoevsky agree that man's alternatives are either God or a universe in which everything is permitted. Such a universe for Dostoevsky can only be a void in which man's freedom is a meaningless and unbearable burden. Sartre, for whom value is always subjective and humanistic, views Nothingness as a kind of building site on which man, because he is free, can reconstruct himself and his world. (Roquentin in *Nausea,* for example, begins to salvage his life only when he recognizes his freedom.) Admittedly, man is in constant flux—he moves from project to project, the value of each surviving only as long as he is committed to it. But if life for Sartre is precarious, and man's most characteristic emotion anguish, Sartre nonetheless offers what little solace there is in a universe without God.

Both Dostoevsky and Camus begin with the assumption that human reason, beyond a certain point, is incapable of answering questions it itself poses—logic leads ultimately to the *absurd*. Rejecting the anarchic rationalism of Underground Man, Dostoevsky resigns himself to the absurd through faith in God, Who comprehends what man cannot. Camus, on the other hand, accepts nothing on faith (he accuses Dostoevsky of "philosophical suicide")—if there is a divine plan behind appearances, it should be accessible to human intelligence. And instead of submitting to the absurd, he advocates revolt. He knows that man can never escape the absurd, or the misery and frustration from which it is inseparable; but through revolt, Camus argues, man can confront the absurd with dignity and thus affirm his value as man. Like Sartre's existentialism, then, Camus' absurd can liberate and revitalize the philosophic skeptic. Limiting revolt at first to an articulation of stoic scorn for the absurd, Camus eventually translates this attitude into an active humanism that succeeds in tempering the adverse effects of the absurd on man.

Sartre and Camus, both professional philosophers, arrive at their philosophic irrationalism through a familiarity with the latest intellectual theories of their day. Genet, without formal education, acquires a similar viewpoint from the extraordinary circumstances of his life. Orphaned at birth, a criminal while still in his teens, he was denied those early childhood influences that are the basis for value of any kind, let alone such absolutes as God. Genet *is* Camus' Absurd Man. His "absurd" is his exile from society. His "revolt," which follows his recognition of the absurd, is his commitment to crime, homosexuality and other deviant patterns. Thus revolt for Genet, as for Camus, becomes a value. But Genet is also Sartre's Existentialist (prompting Sartre to write an entire book about him). For he attempts to consciously reconstruct himself into the criminal par excellence or, failing that, into a poet (the Jean of *Our Lady of the Flowers,* the "I" of *The Thief's Journal*), who lampoons the society that rejected him.

The spiritual bankruptcy of modern man, first in the West and then in the East, is for Malraux only the culmination of a process beginning with the Renaissance, when the concept of God began to lose its significance for Western man. In place of God, the absolute foundation of value and action, there was now only the absurd; and for the unity and certainty of the preceding civilization, only anarchy and anguish. Malraux does not yearn for the return of the lost God, as do Dostoevsky, Kafka and Hesse. Like Sartre, Camus and Genet, he believes that man can rely only on himself. Malraux's humanism, however, has tended to be more collective than either Sartre's or Camus': since the individual is inseparable from the human community, Malraux feels that society itself must be reshaped. Therefore, at least in such early novels as *Man's Fate,* he advocates political action, namely Communism.[2] Communism is a means of correcting the social ills resulting from cultural anarchy; it is also a palliative for anguish, offering its adherents the sense of purpose and dedication that was denied to underground man.

Malraux portrays underground man rejecting God for politics, e.g., the character Ch'en in *Man's Fate* renounces the Biblical God for Communism. Koestler, speaking through Rubashov in *Darkness at Noon,* reverses that movement: he begins with commitment to Communism and ends up discarding it for religious faith. After a decade of active membership in the Communist Party, Koestler is totally disillusioned with it. He is convinced today that Communism not only leads to social and political disaster but that, in addition, it frustrates man's spiritual craving (what Koestler calls the "oceanic sense"). Koestler, like Rubashov, rekindles in himself this longing for the infinite—a reality beyond the materialistic promise of Communism, beyond reason, beyond the known world itself. Marxism is purely secular and rationalistic: its absolute is "historical necessity"; therefore, it cannot fulfill this ontological need in man. Thus, with Koestler's criticism of Communism today, we come full circle to Dostoevsky's denunciation of rational liberalism in 1864.

The eight novels discussed in this book, then, provide a broad survey of underground man. Yet in our concern for him as a general type, we should not lose sight of his rich diversity or the unique genius of each of his creators. In these novels underground man assumes a variety of forms, each one of which is determined by the specific context in which he appears. To dismember a particular work, and then consider only those portions that exemplify underground man, would be an injustice to literary criticism. These novels are works of art (some of them acknowledged masterpieces), in which each part, including underground man, derives its cogency from its tight relationship to the other parts; and underground man comes to

[2] Sartre and Camus put more emphasis on collective action in their later writings. Ironically, Sartre declares himself a Communist today while Malraux has renounced Communism. Camus, though vehemently critical of Communism, did involve himself in political action, particularly during World War II. Genet has generally been indifferent to politics, though in his most recent utterances he has praised the "Third World" revolutionaries.

life only in the concrete detail of each story. Therefore, these works should
be studied in their entirety and in as much detail as is necessary to yield
their full flavor. In the following pages, we shall examine not one but a
variety of underground men, each formed out of conditions that are both
general and unique, and each expressing a vision of life which bears the
unmistakable stamp of a single author.

UNDERGROUND MAN'S BEGINNINGS

Chapter 1

Fyodor Dostoevsky: *Notes from Underground*

Notes from Underground is a philosophic polemic in the form of a personal journal. Dostoevsky portrays the author of the "notes," the unforgettable Underground Man, in the actual process of writing his journal; Underground Man, in turn, is directing his notes to imaginary interlocutors, with whom he carries on a simulated philosophical debate. Although they do not actually say or do anything, he addresses them as "you" and "gentlemen"; and by means of the ideas and sentiments that he attributes to them, they soon take on a definite personality.

In Part I of his notes, Underground Man challenges his opponents by means of direct arguments, which together constitute a rambling essay. In Part II, he ridicules these people indirectly by recounting three incidents from his life, occuring approximately fifteen years before the actual writing of the notes. Only Part II contains the ingredients of the traditional novel (plot, character, setting and so forth), but it would be a mistake to read Part I solely as a philosophic tract. Although the full revelation of Underground Man's personality is deferred to Part II, we feel dramatic tension in almost every line of his monologue in Part I. Though still little more than a voice there, he succeeds nonetheless in creating the illusion of a trial, with his unseen adversaries acting as judge and himself as defendant. For his notes are not merely a journal, like *Steppenwolf* and *Nausea*; they are also a confession, functioning, like much of *Our Lady of the Flowers* and *The Fall,* as "corrective punishment" for the narrator. We are not told the actual cause of Underground Man's guilt until Part II; yet from his first nervous, querulous remarks in Part I, he reveals himself as a haunted man lashing out at the critics who stand in judgement of him.

These "gentlemen" are, in fact, the Nihilists of the Sixties, whom Dostoevsky unceasingly attacked in his later works. Nihilism, a radical development of the rationalism and liberalism of the Enlightenment, was rapidly spreading throughout the Russia of Dostoevsky's day. Rejecting faith for reason and tradition for reform, Nihilism inspired young Russian intellectuals (including Dostoevsky before his imprisonment) who were self-consciously measuring the backwardness of their native Russia against the "progress" in Western Europe. One of the most outstanding spokesmen for this doctrine was N. G. Chernyshevsky, whose *What Is To Be Done?* enjoyed widespread popularity both in czarist and Soviet Russia. But it is possibly even more significant because it was the occasion for the writing of *Notes from Underground.* The immediate target of Dostoevsky's satire is *What Is To Be Done?*, and the imaginary interlocutors whom Underground Man addresses may be taken as a collective embodiment of Chernyshevsky.

Chernyshevsky, who was a visionary Romantic, portrays in *What Is To Be Done?* a modern utopia. The author envisions a radical technology, which would convert the Russian steppes into arable land, produce "palaces" out of glass, and unravel the mysteries of electricity (the time is 1864). Chernyshevsky's social objectives, which would later be expounded by Lenin, include full employment and material abundance, cultivation of the arts, equality of the sexes, and the brotherhood of man. In short, it would be the perfect society, consisting of cheerful, rational men and women who see in their own well-being a pattern of the universal good.

Chernyshevsky constructs his theory out of two basic concepts: the "laws of nature" (as codified by science) and the particular nature of man, which ideally reflects these laws. According to the first assumption, the universe is analogous to a machine, the parts of which are connected in a single chain of cause and effect and function in accordance with a necessary principle, or "law," with predictable regularity. Science has offered man the means of discovering these laws and putting them to practical use, which would require a complete revamping of culture and society. The variable in this equation is man: Will he meet the challenge posed by science, and thus ameliorate his condition? Or will he backslide into the superstition and decadence of the prescientific era?

To answer these questions, Chernyshevsky makes another assumption, borrowed, in vulgarized form, from the English Utilitarians. Man is essentially an animal who, like all natural creatures, is motivated solely by pleasure and pain. What is desirable, and therefore "good," gives pleasure; what is repugnant, and therefore "evil," causes pain. It is in man's nature to seek pleasure, not pain; he suffers only out of ignorance. Once he is able to distinguish what is good from what is harmful, he will automatically choose the good. That he is capable of recognizing his true self-interest is also axiomatic, because man is by nature rational. Man, then, is assured of happiness as long as he uses his reason. "Weigh everything," we are urged. "Choose whatever is useful for you."

What is true of the individual also applies to society as a whole. Society is simply an aggregate of individuals; thus if each man pursues his real self-interest, there results the "greatest good for the greatest number," that is, a happy society. The Utilitarians reject the notion that one man's good requires another man's suffering. It is only the pursuit of our mistaken, as distinguished from our enlightened, self-interest that causes us to inflict pain on others. In the long run, opposition to the common good, like the violation of nature, can only bring us greater suffering than the immediate pleasure it gives us. The proof of this dictum, argues the Utilitarian, lies in the fact that while the pleasure-bent average man covets his neighbor's possessions, his healthy respect for the law keeps him from appropriating them.

Underground Man begins his refutation of Chernyshevsky by comparing the *natural* man (in harmony with the laws of nature) with a bull, whose bellow is always followed by direct action. Such a man need never seek justification, or a "primary" cause, for his action, since he does not see beyond its immediate, or "secondary," cause.[1] For the same reason, he can just as easily abstain from action, just as a charging bull is stopped short by a stone wall. And what is the stone wall? "Why, of course, the laws of nature, the conclusions of natural science, of mathematics." According to the laws of mechanics, one gets a bump on the head if he butts a stone wall, and so the natural man withdraws in proper respect for the absolute, the unchallengeable wall. It is all as simple as two times two equals four.

The complicated Underground Man, on the other hand, cannot act or abstain from action according to so neat a formula. For he is driven by a different set of laws, the "laws of hyperconsciousness." He demands a basic reason for action, a primary as well as a secondary cause. He cannot satisfy

[1] Fyodor Dostoevsky, *Notes from Underground,* tr. Ralph E. Matlaw, New York, 1960. Subsequent quotations from *Notes from Underground* are from this edition.

himself, for example, that revenge is sufficient cause for slapping someone
in the face. He would demand to know why the offender insulted him and
what purpose would be served by his retaliation. And immediately he is
caught up in an infinite regress of cause and effect: if A, then B; if B, then
C, ad infinitum, until all impetus for action has been corroded away by
thought and he sinks into his usual state of "acute inertia":

> Again, in consequence of those accursed laws of consciousness, my
> spite is subject to chemical disintegration. You look into it, the object
> flies off into air, your reasons evaporate, the criminal is not to be
> found, the insult becomes fate rather than an insult. . . .

Conversely, in those rare moments when he is spurred into action but is
suddenly confronted by the wall, he is not so willing to come to a stop as
natural man is. On the contrary, he bangs his head against it, out of pure
spite. Again, he tortures himself with questions. Why should he be limited
by the laws of nature? If they were intended as natural limits to his freedom,
then why was he so built that he desires to rebel against them?—"Of course
I cannot break through a wall by battering my head against it, but I am not
going to resign myself to it simply because it is a stone wall and I am not
strong."

This reply to Chernyshevsky is one of the earliest attacks against the
whole tradition of rationalism and will be echoed by subsequent underground men in the twentieth century. Underground Man's principal
contention is that Chernyshevsky and the Utilitarians commit their greatest error by basing their systems on man's reason. The mainsprings of
action, Underground Man insists, are not rooted in reason, but in desire
and will, in blind impulse, in those chaotic forces which lie beyond the
fringe of consciousness. The intellectuals—including Underground Man,
who reasons himself out of acting—are no less vulnerable to the force of
passion than the unthinking peasant who drinks away his paycheck on
Saturday night and sobers up in jail on Sunday. Reason may point out the
folly of a man's actions. It may offer salutary suggestions for future
behavior. It may even approve his present mode of living. But as a causal
agent of action, argues the skeptical Underground Man, it is insignificant.

The corollary of this conclusion is also obvious, and Underground Man
drives it home with malicious relish: If the individual knowingly acts
against his own interest, will he not be even more likely to thwart the
common good?

> Oh, tell me, who first declared, who first proclaimed, that man only does nasty things because he does not know his own real interests; and that if he were enlightened, if his eyes were opened to his real normal interests, man would at once cease to do nasty things, would at once become good and noble because, being enlightened and understanding his real advantage, he would see his own advantage in the good and nothing else. . . . Oh, the babe! Oh, the pure, innocent child!

In anticipation of Hesse and Camus, Underground Man maintains that history is the record of cruelty and inhumanity, notwithstanding the facile assurances of the Evolutionists, who proclaim that while mankind was morally barbarous in its infancy, it has become progressively more civilized. Underground Man, on the contrary, sees in the millenia only a refinement of man's methods of annihilation, while the essential Adam has remained unchanged.

We are thus incapable of sustained rational behavior, whether for our own good or anybody else's. But even if we could consistently abide by the dictates of reason, Underground Man declares that we "positively ought" to act irrationally, that is, according to impulse, desire and will:

> You see, gentlemen, reason, gentlemen, is an excellent thing, there is no disputing that, but reason is only reason and can only satisfy man's rational faculty, while will is a manifestation of all life, that is, of all human life including reason as well as all impulses. . . .

To live by the rule and measure of the Utilitarians, without tension or conflict, is to renounce our humanity and assume the inert condition of objects. We would have to relinquish "what is most precious and most important—that is, our personality, our individuality"—and become "piano keys" or "organ stops," mechanically responding to the great forces of nature and society. In exchange for a rational existence, we would have to deny our freedom and passion, dull our sense of our own identity, and resign ourselves to the loss of what the modern-day Existentialists have called *authentic* being. Doubtless, the evangelistic fervor of Underground Man's irrationalism is personally motivated—the Utilitarians, after all, are his natural enemy. Nonetheless, it is a timely, if impotent, resistance to powerful currents which began in the eighteenth century, swelled to the breaking point in Dostoevsky's day, and have virtually transformed society since. With the extinction of the individual, Underground Man foresees the grim spectacle of computerized man, which Camus and Koestler will confront three-quarters of a century later.

In their tabulation of what is good for man, the Utilitarians rely on statistics and formulae derived from economics, biology, physics and sociology. They are concerned with collective man, man as a model or an abstraction, and see the individual man as no more than a microcosm of the generalized man. Therefore, they discount "random" deviations from the norm. Possibly, Underground Man does not go as far as Sartre, who maintains that freedom is man's essence. Yet Underground Man, always oriented to the personal, considers individual caprice to be man's "most advantageous advantage," and he insists on "one's own unfettered choice, one's own fancy, however wild it may be, one's fancy worked up at times to frenzy." Chernyshevsky, of course, says a man is free either to reject or conform to the laws of nature. But Underground Man cuts right through this simplistic synthesis of determinism and freedom: if man, constructed in the image of nature, *necessarily* obeys her laws once he recognizes them, then he is not free:

> Bah, gentlemen, what sort of free will is left when we come to tables and arithmetic, when it will all be a case of two times two makes four? Two times two makes four even without my will. As if free will meant that!

Underground Man insists on the freedom to say no, to "put out one's tongue" at the whole new order which Chernyshevsky and the Nihilists attempted to impose on society—the bulging shopping bags, the shining new cottages, the medical and pension funds, the organized leisure, the marvels of the assembly line—all epitomized for Underground Man in the Crystal Palace (an all-glass-and-aluminum structure on exhibit in London in 1851). While Chernyshevsky hails it as the crowning expression of man's genius and inventiveness, Underground Man sees it as nothing more than a building, which merely protects man from the elements, as the anthill does the ant. Progress, then, is an illusion. Science can go on transforming the world indefinitely, yet there will always remain the gaping hole beneath the skin, which even our prehistoric ancestors had to deal with. For unlike the ant, man is a spiritual creature who yearns for something—something beyond the Crystal Palace—which will satisfy the deepest longings of his soul.

But while Underground Man can actually see and touch the things that he despises, he can tell us nothing about his spiritual cravings. In the original text of *Notes from Underground*, he acknowledges the "necessity of faith and Christ." But when for some inexplicable reason the censors deleted this passage, Dostoevsky made no attempt to restore it, perhaps because on second reading of his manuscript he saw that his anti-hero cannot really argue for faith in Christ and at the same time remain an underground man. Indeed, this is the very crux of his problem: he cannot believe in anything. It now becomes clear why Underground Man's reasoning from effect to cause always leads him into the infinite regress—he can never arrive at a limit to the vicious logical process, that is, at the first cause, because God is the first cause and he cannot really believe in God (despite the token allusions he makes to Him). In the rationalistic, utilitarian, nihilistic world portrayed in *Notes from Underground*, he finds little inducement to faith, either in Christ or in anything else; and even when such an inspiration does appear, in the person of Liza the prostitute, it comes too late to have any effect on him. Thus, for all practical purposes, God is dead, although Dostoevsky will resurrect Him in subsequent novels. God is dead not only for Underground Man, who thinks too much, but also for his philistine opponents, who attempt to substitute reason and the laws of nature for Him.

Underground Man is left, then, with two choices: either join Chernyshevsky's contented Utilitarians in the Crystal Palace, or go underground. But if he has chosen underground, it is only as the lesser of two evils:

> Though I have said that I envy the normal man to the point of exasperation, yet I would not care to be in his place as he is now (though I will not stop envying him. No, no; anyway the underground life is more advantageous!) There, at any rate, one can— Bah! But after all, even now I am lying! I am lying because I know myself as surely as two times two makes four, that it is not at all underground that is better, but something different, quite different, for which I long but which I cannot find! Damn underground!

Thus Underground Man concludes at least his formal rebuttal of Chernyshevsky. As the above lines indicate he does hint at the limitations of the life he has chosen, but they are left to the reader's imagination. What really comes through in Part I is the strength of his position, because the only other practical alternative is Chernyshevsky's deceptive utopia. Underground Man himself emerges as a spirited rebel refusing to follow the herd, instead of the lost and desperate man that he really is. Therefore, to comprehend the whole man we must look behind the philosopher's mask and consider such personal details as his physical appearance, his living quarters, his intimate feelings and experiences, and above all, his interaction with other people. While we do get flashes of the real man in Part I, it is only in Part II that he bodies forth as a distinct and complete literary character. Part II also gives us our first glimpse into the specific miseries of an underground existence.

Dostoevsky's hero is appropriate, almost to the point of caricature, to his mode of living. He is a forty-year-old man living in a squalid apartment (his mousehole) in one of the ghettos of St. Petersburg. Short and homely, generally wearing shabby clothes, he is about as prepossessing as a fly, or a mouse, with which he likes to compare himself. He is hypersensitive and neurasthenic and is given to chronic "sickly irritability." He suffers from innumerable ailments, usually psychogenic in origin: migraine headaches, insomnia and a disturbance which he has diagnosed as a liver disease, although he has never seen a doctor. More characteristic of subsequent underground men is his extreme withdrawal and isolation. By the time he writes his journal, he has inherited a small sum of money which allows him to quit a very dull job as a civil servant and assume a life of idleness. He is unmarried and has no immediate family, having been brought up by relatives of whom he makes the briefest mention. He is completely friendless. He belongs to no organizations or institutions, nor does he feel the slightest identification with the Church, the Czar, or the Russian soil. He is, in short, a self-declared exile from human society, with which he maintains only so much contact as is necessary for bare survival.

But if he has rejected the world outside, his apartment is hardly a retreat in which to hoard a few icons in safe seclusion from the vulgar world. It is more like a jail, turning him in upon himself. There he spends long hours daydreaming, imagining himself in "sublime and beautiful" roles that are impossible in "real" life; or he reads Romantic literature and philosophy which, with their emphasis on man's perfectability, he knows to be simply another form of dreaming. Even the "real" situations that take place outside of his room are only a game, though he is always deadly serious in his playacting. For as we have seen, Underground Man ultimately believes in nothing; and the more frenzied his participation in anything, the more hollow his satisfaction. Much of his physical activity—frequenting brothels and other "vile" places—serves no other purpose than to enable him to feel external sensations that might "stifle all that was continually seething" inside of him.

The three main episodes of Part II demonstrate what happens to him when he tries to escape his almost savage solitude and venture out of his room. The first episode begins, appropriately, with a crowd of people, including Underground Man, observing a tavern brawl. Lost in thought and oblivious of the fact that he is blocking the way, he suddenly feels himself lifted up by the shoulders and deposited to one side. The gentleman whose way he had blocked—a tall, muscular, sharply attired army officer—walks on, unaware of Underground Man as anything but an object that had gotten in his way. A moment later, after he manages to shake off his confusion, Underground Man also leaves the scene, and the incident seems to be closed.

But for Underground Man, it has only begun. That night, and all the nights and days for the next two years, he broods about it. He learns all he can about the officer; writes a letter challenging him to a duel (but never sends it); writes a satirical sketch of him (but cannot get it published); stalks him through the streets (but never speaks to him). The closest he comes to any actual contact with the officer is on the narrow sidewalks of the fashionable Nevsky Boulevard; yet even here he steps aside for him, just as the officer on his part makes way for generals and other personages of high rank. Finally, after two years of obsession with the officer, he decides upon his "revenge": the next time he encounters the officer on the sidewalk, he will not give way to him, even if he has to bump into him. To carry out his plan, he borrows money and purchases a wardrobe, which he feels will give him courage; he carefully works out the details of his scheme, repeatedly visiting the spot where he will carry it off. But when the crucial moment comes, predictably he makes way for the officer again. After several such unsuccessful attempts, he decides to give up his plan. But immediately afterwards, he encounters the officer again, and instantly—without a moment's thought—he closes his eyes and runs head-on into him. And this time, the officer affair is definitely closed.

What this incident most dramatically exemplifies is the cleavage in Underground Man between action and thought. The natural man, in his place, would have responded instantly to the insult. Underground Man's reaction, on the other hand, is delayed. He takes the insult home to brood on, and we can imagine from his many sleepless nights the agony he goes through: the tortured self-recriminations and rationalizations, the compulsive recollections of the incident, the endless analysis of motives, the speculations as to what might have been done. Clearly he feels insulted; but from prolonged inertia he has lost the habit, if indeed he ever had it, of responding in the right manner and at the right moment. He repeatedly demonstrates that while he is capable of both reason and action, for him the two are not necessarily connected. His ultimate revenge does not easily and naturally follow from his rational preparations; it happens in spite of them, that is, by pure accident, since he actually gives up his plan moments before he executes it.

He acts; but his actions, like those of the Existentialist and Absurdist, do not derive their justification from their apparent purpose. What precipitates him into motion is not his commitment to a code of honor, for deep down inside of him honor, like all absolutes, has no meaning. Rather, it is his elemental, almost organic, need for action *for its own sake.* To be human is to be active, and the officer's provocation serves as a kind of catalyst to momentarily rouse the sedentary Underground Man from his dreams and his books. Revenge becomes an end in itself, long after the original insult has been forgotten. In effect, it is a game, a surrogate reality of Underground Man's own creation, a ritual in which he can go through the motions of "real" living while remaining underground. But as for what happens afterwards, he tells us, " . . . if you read my first chapter, 'Underground,' you can guess for yourself." What we can guess is that he really derives little satisfaction from his sham triumph over the officer. For the hyperconscious Underground Man—the first of the many role players we will be examining—knows all the while that he is only playing the buffoon in a theatrical farce. Though he continues to "thumb his nose" at Chernyshevsky's Crystal Palace, his actions remain those of a frustrated man.

The second major episode of Part II concerns itself with another of his sorties into the world of men. His solitude having become unendurable, he resolves to make one of his rare social calls. But since he has no current friends, he must fall back on the company of a group of his former school chums, between himself and whom there exists only a mutual dislike. In spite of this fact, he invites himself to a going-away party they are planning for another schoolfellow, one Zverkov, whom Underground Man also hates. On the following evening, they all meet in a hotel room. There is an initial exchange of insults between Underground Man and the others; then they simply ignore him for the rest of the evening. For three hours they sit at one end of the room while he paces the floor at the other, literally getting drunker by the minute. Finally, after a parting exchange of insults between him and them, they go off, presumably to a brothel. In a drunken rage, he starts off after them, determined to slap Zverkov in the face. But when he arrives at the brothel, he discovers they have gone elsewhere, and he is left to console himself with one of the inmates of the house.

We naturally wonder why Underground Man thrusts himself upon a group of people with whom he knows he cannot get along, and why he insists on remaining with them despite the suffering they subject him to. Clearly, he is held to them in spite of himself, just as he felt compelled to address himself to their counterparts, the interlocutors, in Part I. He is agonizingly aware of how absurd it is for him to associate himself with Zverkov and his friends, yet that knowledge itself only impels him more inevitably toward them:

> But what made me furious was that I knew for certain that I would go, that I would purposely go; and the more tactless, the more ill-mannered my going would be, the more certainly I would go.

As usual, his motivations here are so complicated as almost to defy analysis. Certainly, loneliness and boredom are factors: reunion with his schoolmates, if only to give them battle, is at least a change. Contact with other human beings is a necessary mode of realizing himself; like looking into a mirror or rereading something he has written, it is a kind of feedback that confronts him with himself. Finally, it enables him to burst out of the cocoon that he has woven around himself; he experiences with his companions a galvanization, the more so as they incite him to combat. The questions they put to him, the repartee they draw him into, the occasion itself—all demand that he assume some definite identity, some specific form, which his many years underground have blurred beyond recognition. He, of course, leaps to the challenge, for it offers him another role to play. And, as usual, the identity he assumes is perversely adapted to his audience.

Zverkov and the others are exemplifications of Chernyshevsky's Utilitarianism as viewed through the prism of Dostoevsky's satire. Ambitious, calculating and crude, they are all motivated by the one passion, success in the world. Even as children they had begun laying plans for securing a comfortable berth in the civil service or the army. Already they were attaching themselves to what would be useful to them and ruthlessly rejecting anything and anybody that did not further their advantage. Thus Underground Man, even had he himself been less obnoxious, would always have been an object of their disdain; for it was quite plain to everybody that, despite his excellence at his studies, he would never distinguish himself in the "real" world—the service, the professions or high society. Zverkov, on the other hand, was always the shining idol of the group because of the money behind him. All but Underground Man vied with one another for his notice, not because of any tangible favors he might confer on them, but because attachment to him was an honor in itself. Since his schooldays, time has only added to Zverkov's luster. He has come into his estate and is richer and more arrogant than ever; he has advanced in the army, partially through his own efforts, but mostly through his family's influence; and, according to his boasts, he is a perfect wonder with the women, though he will soon be ready to make the proper match and settle down to his country estate. He has not reached the age of thirty; yet he is already callous, jaded and cynical toward everything except his easy success in the world.

What must be emphasized, however, is that Zverkov and his immediate admirers are not isolated cases. Dostoevsky believed that their utilitarian outlook was rapidly becoming characteristic of that whole frantic society which found inspiration in a book like *What Is To Be Done?* But if they are representative, then his satirical portrait of them can only strengthen our sympathy for Underground Man. What choice does he, or any young middleclass Russian of the day, have? Unless he becomes a monk or chooses to become a peasant (like the visionary Tolstoy), he ordinarily goes into business, the civil service, the army, or the professions—all of which encourage ambition, competitiveness and self-interest. Underground Man, however, is not religious; and, like subsequent underground men, he belongs not to the soil but to the cold and friendless city, which is characterized in the novel by the "wet, yellow, dingy snow." Therefore, as dismal as it is, he chooses underground.

Yet we should not conclude from this that his ultimate choice is determined by moral scruples. To be sure, he expresses a loathing for Zverkov's values with the drunken toast: " . . . I hate phrases, phrasemongers and corseted waists . . . I love truth, sincerity and honesty . . . thought . . . true comradeship . . . ." But, ironically, Underground Man too is a phrasemonger, and his phrases are certainly not to be taken as an accurate description of himself. As we have seen in the incident with the officer, he may take up a principle momentarily and even act in accordance with it. But he has no enduring belief in it. He has only taken it up because it is consistent with the role he is playing at the moment; and when in the next moment he drops the role, he also discards the principle. Since the only way he can interact with people is to antagonize them, the role he assumes here is that of the man of sentiment, the Romantic exponent of the sublime and the beautiful, because that figure is the antithesis of utilitarian Zverkov.

But if Underground Man is not genuinely committed to any expressed absolute, he does have real desires, however fluctuating they may be. Certainly another of his motives for clinging to his schoolfellows is his fundamental insistence that they take notice of him; and the more vile and outrageous his behavior, the more urgent his demand for attention. One of his innumerable, contradictory desires is that he and Zverkov establish a friendship, though he knows that he could not abide such a friendship even if it were possible. He harbors an elementary fear that he will be forgotten in his mousehole; and though he has chosen his own exile, he finds society's indifference to him intolerable. He plays on the conscience of Zverkov and his friends and, by implication, society—like the man who suffers from a toothache and who, through his incessant moans, deliberately inflicts that suffering on everyone else around him. Like the heroes of *Nausea, The Fall* and *Our Lady of the Flowers,* he will not be ignored. The merrymakers try to ignore him at the party and thus drive him away. He vows instead to

> . . . sit on to the end . . . you would be pleased, my friends, if I left. Nothing will induce me to go. I'll go on sitting here, and drinking to the end, on purpose, as a sign that I don't attach the slightest importance to you. I will go on sitting and drinking, because this is a public-house and I paid my entrance money. I'll sit here and drink. . . .

On the morning after, however, Underground Man's vow goes the way of all his resolutions. He writes a short note of apology to his erstwhile companions, taking full blame for the disastrous evening while generously exonerating his tormentors. Then he simply forgets about them. The apology, of course, hardly expresses his true feelings. Again, he is affecting the sublime and beautiful pose, for it would certainly be more natural for him to brood a few years over this affront as he did in the preceding episode. But a new threat has intervened, plunging him into such a profound anxiety that Zverkov and his companions lose all significance beside it. His new concern is the prostitute Liza, and so begins the third episode of Part II.

Arriving at the brothel and not finding Zverkov, he consoles himself by taking Liza to bed. Afterwards, still smarting from the humiliation that Zverkov caused him, he resolves to avenge himself on her by making her feel guilty for being a prostitute. He describes to her the grim end she must come to while painting a pretty picture of family life, which she must forgo as a whore. Beginning to believe his own fabrications, he waxes so eloquent in his descriptions of marital bliss that he finally succeeds in making Liza feel remorse for her present life and disgust for herself. He assures her, however, that she can count on him for help should she choose to renounce that life, and before he leaves he gives her his address.

A few days later she does leave the brothel and, full of gratitude and love, goes straight to Underground Man, whom she considers her savior. He becomes hysterical: he proceeds to insult her, sadistically pointing out to her that he did not mean a word of what he said and that he had only wanted to make her suffer because of the suffering Zverkov had caused him. But when he breaks down and tearfully begins to confess his self-loathing and almost genuine sorrow—again, playacting becomes reality—he manages only to generate greater love and sympathy in her. She embraces him; but this arouses in him a new feeling of "mastery and possession," and so he takes her to bed again. We do not know the particulars of their lovemaking, except that he now "insulted her once and for all." Yet he attempts one more insult: he hands her a five-ruble note as she is leaving. When he discovers, moments later, that she has tossed it to the floor, he runs out after her, prepared to fall at her feet. But she is nowhere in sight, and Part II closes with Underground Man staring into the dark night, contemplating the wet and dingy snow.

This incident is both the ostensible and the most significant link between Parts I and II. Liza is the cause of that guilt which was hinted at in the first part. Her memory haunts him, even now, fifteen years later; it was to shake it off that he decided to write his notes, that is, his confession. If the incident does not actually seal Underground Man's doom, it at least defines it, once and for all, leaving no doubt either in his mind or the reader's as to how he will spend the rest of his days. In this episode, his confusion between make-believe and reality, his compulsion to seek out people and then strike out at them when they get too close, his arbitrary assumption of a position one moment and his equally arbitrary rejection of it the next, the constant tension between reason and impulse, his desperate self-assertion followed by his total self-debasement—all the skeins of his tangled personality—are brought together into a single, horrifying image.

Like the other episodes, this one throws into stark relief Underground Man's inability to establish meaningful human relations. But there is a difference. We can hardly blame him for despising Zverkov and the first officer, and his experience with them does not exclude the possibility that some rare soul may yet come along and break through his isolation. But when he rejects the gentle and profoundly sympathetic Liza, we know all hope is gone, especially as his savagery and cruelty increase with the intensity of her love: "... I was a despicable man, and what is more, incapable of loving her." Like the prostitute Sonia's love for Raskolnikov in *Crime and Punishment,* Liza's could conceivably redeem the lost soul of Underground Man. But whereas that great sinner, Raskolnikov, eventually asks for Sonia's cross, Underground Man is beyond redemption. Fully aware that Liza is his last hope, he nonetheless cannot, or will not, accept her offer of love, thus grimly refuting once more the Utilitarian assumption that when we once see our true self-interest, we can, and will, pursue it.

Dostoevsky offers various psychological reasons for his protagonist's incapacity to love or be loved: he never knew true love as a child; ordinarily frustrated in his attempts at self-assertion by sturdy fellows like Zverkov and the officer, he invariably attempts to dominate and tyrannize over the occasional friend that comes his way; enclosed within his self-contained universe, he is incapable of making the accommodation that love for another person demands. But Dostoevsky, despite his prodigious understanding of psychological motives, is always interested in the metaphysical basis for his characters' actions. Love is predicated on faith: the willingness to give total assent to what is only partially comprehended. But this is precisely what Underground Man is incapable of doing.

A child of his times, he insists on a rational justification for action, even though he devotes pages of argument in Part I to deny that such justification is possible and, in Part II, goes on to demonstrate the truth of his argument. To be sure, he has the impulse to love Liza. When, in the brothel, he sings the praises of love and marriage to her in order to torment her, he actually ends up by believing what he is saying—what begins as parody ends as a literal expression of a heartfelt need. Likewise, when he runs into the snow after the departed Liza, his one passion is to overtake her and beg her forgiveness. But like all of his impulses, the impulse to love Liza is short-lived, quickly checked by reason or supplanted by another impulse. Instead of pursuing her, he rationalizes himself into a state of immobility:

> To fall down before her, to sob with remorse, to kiss her feet, to beg her forgiveness! I longed for that. My whole heart was being rent to pieces, and never, never will I recall that moment with indifference. But—what for? I thought. Would I not begin to hate her, perhaps, even tomorrow, just because I had kissed her feet today? Would I give her happiness? Had I not again recognized that day, for the hundredth time, what I was worth? Would I not torment her?

It matters not whether he reasons first that life with Liza is impossible, and then rejects her, or whether deep down inside of him he denies her first and then finds the rational justification for that denial. Reason, in any event, is a melancholy ally. As with later underground men, it is easier for him to deny than to affirm, even when he has nothing to lose and everything to gain. He cannot simply let himself go with Liza; he cannot freely love. And primarily for that reason he, like other loveless protagonists, remains captive to underground.

Underground Man may be the neurotic par excellence, as so many of Dostoevsky's characters are. But it would be a mistake to see in Dostoevsky's writings nothing more than a pre-Freudian survey of abnormal psychology. His characters often appear grotesque through the lens of the realist; yet they are actually composites of attitudes and traits which are common, not only to underground men, but to all of us. As Dostoevsky's footnote to the novel shows, Underground Man is not an isolated case, but one of the inevitable "representatives of the current generation," and by extension, our own. At the conclusion of the novel, Underground Man anticipates his interlocutors' attempt to shrug off his notes as a personal record without general significance. But Underground Man—and here he is clearly speaking for Dostoevsky—does not let them off that easily:

> As for what concerns me in particular I have only, after all, in my life carried to an extreme what you have not dared to carry halfway, and what's more, you have taken your cowardice for good sense, and have found comfort in deceiving yourselves. So that perhaps, after all, there is more "life" in me than in you. Look into it more carefully! After all, we don't even know where living exists now, what it is, and what it is called! Leave us alone without books and we will be lost and in a

confusion at once—we will not know what to join, what to cling to, what to love and what to despise. We are even oppressed by being men—men with real individual body and blood. We are ashamed of it, we think it a disgrace and try to contrive to be some sort of impossible generalized man.

Thus, by a curious twist, Underground Man and his imaginary opponents of Part I end up in the same camp. Like them, he is first and foremost an intellectual, who attempts to confine experience within a theoretical framework devoid of passion and impulse. He expresses loathing for cold, calculating reason while his interlocutors hold it up as man's chief asset; yet the roles he plays, particularly with Liza, are often just as artificial and inhuman as Chernyshevsky's robot. Though he is irrational in his behavior, in his thinking at least he pushes reason even beyond the safe and practical limits which the Utilitarians set to it. It is perhaps this stubborn lucidity and the anguish that accompanies it which most sharply set him off from the others. By contrast to the fatuous interlocutors, he sees his terrible position for what it is and has pronounced irrevocable judgement upon himself.

UNDERGROUND MAN
AND GOD

Chapter 2

Franz Kafka: *The Castle*

Kafka's futile pursuit of logic leads him into a world as absurd as Dostoevsky's. His novel *The Trial* begins with the line, "Someone must have traduced Joseph K., for without having done anything wrong he was arrested one fine morning" and, without ever being told his crime or confronted with his accuser, he is executed. The condemned prisoners of "In the Penal Colony," whose guilt (like Joseph K.'s) is never questioned, are executed by means of a machine which literally carves the name of their assumed, but never proven, crime on their backs. Georg in "The Judgment," who is unexpectedly "sentenced" by his father to death by drowning, instantly plunges to a watery death, his last words being "Dear parents, I have always loved you, all the same." Gregor Samsa in "Metamorphosis" wakes up one morning to find himself transformed into a giant insect; his parents and sister, whom he has supported at the sacrifice of his own happiness, renounce him because of his metamorphosis while he, in order to further accommodate them, quietly dies. The humanlike animal in "The Burrow," who has spent most of his life constructing an under-the-ground fortress against his enemies, suddenly begins to hear noises which grow progressively louder and which portend his imminent destruction. The villagers in "The Great Wall of China," who also have enemies, build themselves a "protective" wall with openings in it large enough to admit invading armies. Through somebody's error, the dead hunter Gracchus, in the story by that name, sails eternally on the ghostly ship which was to convey him to the other world.

Kafka's fictional world is unmistakable. On the surface, it combines Chaplinesque farce with the Theatre of the Absurd and is peopled with grotesque Dickensian characters. Strangers peer through one's bedroom window as a matter of course, and their snickers and whispers follow him down interminable, dark, winding corridors that end in a cul de sac. Ill-formed young teen-age girls leer at him and invite him to seduce them. Adults indulge in the antics of children, children utter the worldly wisdom (and cynicism) of the ancients. What is noble and sublime conceals itself behind the sordid: the law courts are in tenement houses; official interrogations are conducted in taverns; corrupt couriers carry tidings from the gods. To the unsuspecting reader, Kafka's world seems deranged, defying common sense and the laws of probability. Time and distance are distorted. The incredible is treated as if it were the most ordinary of circumstances, the ordinary can suddenly develop into a crisis. The simplest situation turns out to be extraordinarily complicated, permitting innumerable yet contradictory interpretations. Logic labors in vain, effort is circular. Kafka's world is ridiculous, full of hilarious contretemps; but the hilarity is always enveloped by a pervasive gloom, and somewhere in the background, yet never too far away, hovers a palpable though unseen menace.

If Kafka's stories follow the bizarre pattern of a dream, it is because he sought to portray through them his own "dreamlike inner life."[1] Writing was for Kafka a personal necessity, as it was for Genet after him. It was a release, a form of therapy, a means of warding off madness. In one of his diary entries, Kafka confesses to his "great yearning to write all of my anxiety out of me, write it into the depths of the paper just as it comes out of the depths of me. . . . "[2] Kafka did not simply create imaginary underground men, as did Dostoevsky, Hesse, Sartre, Camus, Malraux and Koestler. Like Genet, he projected into his fictional characters his own underground dilemma, which he was never to resolve either as a writer or as a man. While it is true that Kafka was not literally his characters (including the suggestive K.'s of *The Trial* and *The Castle*), the term Kafkaesque applies as much to him as it does to them.

Yet nowhere throughout his fiction does he expound his "philosophy": there is a *Kafkaesque* condition or situation, but not Kafkaism; and his fiction leaves us not with the answers to the questions it poses but with the bafflement of the questioner. Kafka himself seems to have been aware of the

[1] *Diaries of Franz Kafka (1914-1923)*, Max Brod, ed., tr. Martin Greenburg, New York, 1948, p. 77.
[2] *Diaries of Franz Kafka* (1910-1913), Max Brod, ed., tr. Joseph Kresh, New York, 1948, p. 173.

ineffable element in his writings when he wrote, in one of his aphorisms, that the "inner world can only be experienced, not described."[3] Meaning in his stories is always only suggested—through situation or setting or description—and even then it is less a paraphraseable statement than an intricate and undefinable mood.

For a direct statement of Kafka's personal beliefs, we must turn to his autobiographical writings, the most remarkable of which is the *Letter to His Father*. In the *Letter*, Kafka, with an astounding astuteness and precision and an explicitness totally absent from his fiction, analyzes his complex relationship to his father, Hermann Kafka, the earliest, the profoundest, and the most lasting force in Franz's life. For if writing was an expression of his psychic life (particularly of his anxiety), it was also an attempt to deal with his father:

> My writing was all about you; all I did there, after all, was to bemoan what I could not bemoan upon your breast. It was an intentionally long-drawn-out leave-taking from you, only although it was brought about by force on your part, it did take its course in the direction determined by me.[4]

Thus through writing Kafka hoped to free himself both of his father and of his anxiety. By implication, the father was at the core of his inner being and, in all probability, the basic cause of his anxiety. He was, in short, the primal reason why Franz Kafka became an underground man.

Hermann Kafka was everything that Franz could not, or would not, be. In the *Letter* Franz writes:

> Sometimes I imagine the map of the world spread out flat and you stretched out diagonally across it. And what I feel then is that only those territories come into question for my life that either are not covered by you or are not within your reach. (*Letter,* p. 115)

Given the magnitude of the father's impact on Franz, the latter felt himself as virtually excluded from the ordinary world. Hermann Kafka was strong and in excellent health, extroverted, domineering, successful in business despite his humble beginnings, active in the Jewish community of Prague,

---

[3] Franz Kafka, "The Eight Octavo Notebooks," in *Wedding Preparations in the Country,* tr. Ernst Kaiser and Eithne Wilkins, London, 1954, p.72.

[4] Franz Kafka, *Letter to His Father,* tr. Ernst Kaiser and Eithne Wilkins, New York, 1970, p. 87.

and a totally secure husband and father. In classic contrast to his father, Franz was sickly throughout his life, dying of tuberculosis at the age of forty. He was gentle, sensitive, intense, and inclined to withdraw (despite the considerable attraction he exerted on his friends); a Jew living in Prague and immersed in German culture, he was at heart neither Jew, nor Czech, nor German. Notwithstanding the esteem in which he was held at the Workmen's Accident Insurance Institution, where he was employed for many years, he viewed that work as a dreary necessity which kept him from writing, and he even considered suicide at one point to free himself of it. Finally, though he held marriage and family to be the highest of human achievements ("A man without a wife is not a human being"), he despaired of ever marrying because marriage, more than anything else, was the father's "intimate domain."

As a child, Kafka considered his father nothing short of a superman and viewed himself as a lowly creature for whom the father felt only contempt. Possibly this feeling about himself in relation to the father had its origins in a childhood experience which Franz recounts in the *Letter,* an experience which did him "inner harm" and from which he was never to recover. One night, to silence Franz's whimpering, Hermann Kafka snatched the child out of bed, carried him to the porch, and left him there in his nightshirt. For the astonished Franz, unable to connect logically his misdeed with the punishment, this incident was traumatic:

> Even years afterwards I suffered from the tormenting fancy that the huge man, my father, the ultimate authority, would come almost for no reason at all and take me out of bed in the night and carry me out to the *pavlatche* [porch], and that therefore I was such a mere nothing for him. (*Letter,* p. 17)

With this event, and numerous others in which the father expressed what the child could only read as scorn, Franz acquired what was to be a lifelong sense of guilt:

> I had lost my self-confidence where you were concerned, and in its place had developed a boundless sense of guilt. (In recollection of this boundlessness I once wrote of someone, accurately: "He is afraid the shame will outlive him, even.") (*Letter,* p. 73)[5]

---

[5] Kafka's reference is to the closing line of *The Trial.* In that novel Joseph K. is summoned out of his bed and placed under arrest.

Like Gregor in "Metamorphosis," Franz felt as if he were some kind of vermin, never forgetting his father's taunt when the latter disapproved of Franz's friends: "He who lies down with dogs gets up with fleas." He became indecisive, self-effacing, convinced in advance that he would fail at whatever he put his hand to (in spite of his very real accomplishments throughout his life). He suffered from insomnia or was often visited by nightmares. And he was obsessed with the idea of judgment and punishment, believing that "One was so to speak punished before one even knew that one had done something bad." (*Letter,* p. 37) Like Joseph K., he lived under the continual anxiety of a man on trial, with his father in the role of judge. He says in the *Letter*:

> Hence the world was for me divided into three parts: one, in which I, the slave, lived under laws that had been invented only for me and which I could, I did not know why, never completely comply with; then a second world, which was infinitely remote from mine, in which you lived, concerned with government, with the issuing of orders and with annoyance about their not being obeyed; and finally a third world where everybody else lived happily and free from orders and from having to obey. (*Letter,* p. 29)

The father was inaccessible or deaf to the child's feeble protests, which Franz soon stopped making. Nor was there a third party who could intercede for him. His mother was generally ineffective or "allied" herself to the father, for whom she played the part of "beater during the hunt," discouraging Franz from any healthy defiance of his father.

Even without the mother's interference, however, it is highly improbable that the youthful Franz would ever seriously have challenged his father. For he had too much admiration (in his words, "veneration") for the father, and too much contempt for himself. Of course, as the adult who wrote the *Letter,* Franz saw his father for what he actually was: insensitive, arbitrary and egotistical; and he could write of him, "For me you took on the enigmatic quality that all tyrants have whose rights are based on their person and not on reason." Yet in spite of his lucidity in the *Letter,* Franz continually qualifies his criticism of his father, either finding excuses for him or assuring him that if the father were to blame, the son was even more at fault. Kafka pushes fairness to exasperating lengths in the *Letter* because there, as in his other writings, he attempts to express conflicting emotions.

Kafka's early childhood would doubtless make fascinating reading in abnormal psychology. Yet a strictly psychological approach to the study of the man and his works would only touch the surface. His ultimate preoccupations were metaphysical and theological (subtly couched in symbolism in his fiction). Psychology, he warns, is only "the description of the reflection of the terrestrial world in the heavenly plane. . . ." ("Notebooks," p. 72) Therefore, it is not his childhood experiences as such that should concern us but how Franz Kafka, the writer and thinker, transformed them into a comprehensive world view that went beyond the individual Franz Kafka and his immediate family. What we discover when we leave the *Letter* and turn to his other nonfictional utterances (the aphorisms, diaries and conversations) are subtle refinements of the initial themes of the *Letter*. Franz Kafka has assumed both the essential condition of Everyman, unchanged from Creation, and the shadowy form of a contemporary misfit. Hermann Kafka has been absorbed into larger images of authority, e.g., institutions, government, society and ultimately God.

Kafka's attitude toward his father is best reflected in his relationship to God. Contrary to Hesse and Dostoevsky, he had ambivalent feelings about God. On the one hand, God and eternity are tangible realities, coextensive with man and the world of time. ("To every instant there is a correspondence in something outside of time.")[6] One is therefore a "traitor to himself" if he does not believe in the "significant interrelation of all things and all moments, in the eternal existence of life as a single whole, in what is nearest and what is farthest."[7] On the other hand, God plays games with us:

> The animal wrests the whip from its master and whips itself in order
> to become master, not knowing that this is only a fantasy produced by
> a new knot in the master's whip-lash. ("Reflections," p. 41)

Faith in Him is joyless:

> How much more oppressive than the most inexorable conviction of
> our present sinful state is even the weakest conviction of the coming
> eternal justification of our temporality. Only strength in the en-
> durance of this second conviction, which in its purity entirely
> comprehends the first, is the measure of faith. ("Reflections," p. 50)

[6] "Reflections on Sin, Suffering, Hope and the True Way," in *Wedding Preparations in the Country*, tr. Ernst Kaiser and Eithne Wilkins, London, 1954, p. 90.
[7] Gustav Janouch, *Conversations With Kafka*, selection published in *Encounter*, August, 1971, pp. 21-22.

Faith is also exacting:

> . . . knowledge of Good and Evil is both a step leading up to eternal
> life and an obstacle in the way. If you want to attain eternal life after
> having gained knowledge—and you will not be able to do otherwise
> than want it, for knowledge of Good and Evil *is* this will—you will
> have to destroy yourself, the obstacle, in order to build the step, which
> is the destruction. Expulsion from Paradise was thus not an act but a
> happening. ("Notebooks," p. 100)

And faith may very well prove futile:

> The Messiah will come only when he is no longer necessary, he will
> come only one day after his arrival, he will not come on the last day,
> but on the last day of all. ("Notebooks," p. 88)

Kafka rejected institutionalized Judaism. Yet he passionately believed in
the fundamental Hebraic premise of the Fall. Human life for him was a
protracted exile, an agonizing trek through the desert, with Paradise
behind us and God before us, and both receding in proportion to the effort
we make to reach them: "We are separated from God on two sides: the
Fall separates us from him, the Tree of Life separates him from us."
("Notebooks," p. 96) Unlike the Biblical chronicler, however, Kafka did
not claim to know how man had transgressed, though he did assume that
man—at least Kafka[8]—was guilty. Nor did he believe that rituals of
atonement or a given way of life guaranteed redemption, though by all
accounts his personal life was highly ethical. God for him was inscrutable,
and since He was so removed from us, it was futile to ask Him questions.
But whether from hope or perversity, Kafka could not resign himself to
the divine silence:

> Previously I did not understand why I got no answer to my question,
> today I do not understand how I could believe I was capable of asking.
> But I didn't really believe, I only asked. ("Reflections," pp. 41-42)

Kafka might actually have been happier had he been able to deny God's
existence. To be sure, he did not conceive of Him as an evil, Manichaean

---

[8] The narrator of "Investigations of a Dog" suggests that we suffer from a racial guilt because our ancestors "strayed from the Word."

deity whose assigned role was to torment mankind—he was too respectful of Omnipotence, too inclined to belittle his own understanding, to make such a presumption. For the same reasons, he did not rebel, as Camus did. Kafka had already accepted guilt—guilt for him was always a foregone conclusion. Besides, revolt against the Absolute could only be ludicrous:

> The crows maintain that a single crow could destroy the heavens. There is no doubt of that, but it proves nothing against the heavens, for heaven simply means: the impossibility of crows. ("Reflections," p. 41)

Nonetheless, one suspects that Kafka, in all humility, resented God.

Of course, it would be an oversimplification to ascribe Kafka's curious blend of faith and pessimism solely to his relations with his father. There is, after all, his marginal position as a Jew (though even this he blames his father for). On the one hand, the link between his metaphysics and Judaism is self-evident; on the other hand, an orthodox Jew would be outraged by Kafka's conclusions. Nor is Kafka the only important writer who has lamented his severance from the Father (both literal and symbolic). This theme is a bulwark of modern literature, spanning roughly a century from Dostoevsky to Camus. Kafka's writing is indeed personal. Yet he speaks for all men, and particularly for that species of contemporary man whom we have thus far identified as underground man:

> I have brought nothing with me of what life requires, so far as I know, but only the universal human weakness. With this—in this respect it is gigantic strength—I have vigorously absorbed the negative element of the age in which I live, an age that is, of course, very close to me, which I have no right ever to fight against, but as it were a right to represent. The slight amount of the positive, and also of the extreme negative, which capsizes into the positive, are something in which I have had no hereditary share. I have not been guided into life by the hand of Christianity—admittedly now slack and failing—as Kierkegaard was, and have not caught the hem of the Jewish prayer-mantle—now flying away from us—as the Zionists have. I am an end or a beginning. ("Notebooks," p. 114)

Whatever its origins, Kafka's conception of man cut off from ultimate authority is reflected both in his relations with his father and in the bulk of his stories. In such early works as "The Judgment" and "Metamorphosis," the rift is literally between father and son, in which the formidable father first rejects and then destroys the pathetic son. In subsequent tales authority is expanded and refined. In "The Great Wall of China," it becomes the High Command, issuing incomprehensible decrees to a whole nation; in "In the Penal Colony," the dead Commandant, inspiring fear even from his grave, from which he may one day rise without warning; in *The Trial,* the many-tentacled Law, relentlessly singling out the "guilty" and dispatching a justice that baffles common sense. In all of these stories the Absolute is beyond human reach, yet it is everywhere within the human world and nothing is free of it. Ineluctable, arbitrary, mysterious and seemingly irrational, it appears to be of tangible benefit to no one; if anything, it thwarts human effort. Yet reality for Kafka would be inconceivable without it.

As for the suppliants in these later stories, they are occasionally ordinary citizens (a whole populace in "The Great Wall of China"). For the most part, however, they are outcasts (e.g., the prisoners in "In the Penal Colony" or the termagant hermit in "The Burrow"). They might simply have been an inconspicuous bourgeois who suddenly falls out of grace, such as Joseph K. in *The Trial,* or a shade that belongs neither to the living nor to the dead, such as the unburied Gracchus in "The Hunter Gracchus." Generally, Kafka's heroes wear the mark of Cain. They have a special relationship with the Absolute that distinguishes them from everyone else (the "third world" of the *Letter*). Their destiny may be imposed on them, as in the case of Joseph K. or Gracchus. More likely, it is chosen, by for example the protagonist of "Investigations of a Dog," who spends his life vainly seeking the source of the "heavenly music" he heard in his youth, or the artist in "The Hunger Artist," who starves himself because he wishes to eat only heavenly food. They are modern-day Don Quixotes, possibly because, as the protagonist of "Investigations of a Dog" says, ". . . if the faint hope that we still possess should give way to complete hopelessness, the attempt is still worth the trial, since you do not desire to live as you are compelled to live." And inevitably, they inflict on themselves what the narrator of "The Burrow" describes as the "punishment for some sin I do not know of."

We should hardly be surprised to find this same pattern in Kafka's last major work, *The Castle.* Power in this novel belongs to an elite hierarchy secreting itself in a mysterious mountain castle and exerting absolute control over the village below. Although various villagers make their moderate appeals to the Castle, it is a stranger named K. who makes the most pressing demands upon it. Having been hired as a land surveyor for the Castle, K. has made the long and arduous journey to the village only to discover that no such position exists. Throughout the novel, he makes repeated futile attempts to communicate with the Castle, first to clarify his situation, but soon simply to be granted an interview with someone there. Scarcely acknowledging his existence, the Castellans deny him admittance to the Castle, although they do finally give him official permission to reside in the town. But this indulgence comes to him only as he lies dying of exhaustion from his very attempts to reach the Castle. Moreover, it is tendered to him in so ungracious a fashion as to seem less an act of grace than an insult; for he is told that he is being allowed to stay in the village not because of any legal claim or meritorious effort on his part, but because of "certain auxiliary circumstances."[9]

Both Castle and village are situated on a remote mountain, which effectively cuts them off from the rest of the world. The bleak weather adds to their isolation. Winter is the only real season (spring and summer are often only two days long, during which time it rains). Cold winds and snowdrifts batter the tiny hamlet. Its streets are generally deserted, especially after dark, and it is dark for all but a few hours of the day. The Castle itself looms directly over the village; but access to it is difficult. The main street of town, as if to tease the curious sightseer, seems continually to draw nearer to the Castle, yet always skirts it (" . . . though it did not lead away from the Castle, it led no nearer to it either"). Because of the excessive mist and darkness, the Castle is usually concealed, but in the brief periods of sunlight it reveals itself as a sprawling, inhospitable cluster of buildings, peeling with age. The Castle is inseparable from the village, yet it is supremely independent:

> When K. looked at the Castle, often it seemed to him as if he were observing someone who sat quietly there gazing in front of him, not lost in thought and so oblivious of everything, but free and un- troubled, as if he were alone with nobody to observe him, and yet must notice that he was observed, and all the same remained with his

[9] Kafka never finished the novel. However, on the basis of what he is supposed to have told his friend and biographer, Max Brod, scholars have assumed that he had intended to end it with K.'s death and the belated indulgence from the Castle.

calm not even slightly disturbed; and really – one did not know whether it was cause or effect – the gaze of the observer could not remain
concentrated there, but slid away.[10]

The village is apparently like any other town, with its own mayor and
city council, and we never know precisely what the Castle does. But
nothing, however insignificant, escapes its scrutiny or can survive very long
without its official or tacit approval. Final decisions are made by a formidable
echelon of officials, who remain aloof from the townsfolk. Direct dealing
with the villagers is carried on by deputies, or Secretaries, who, to protect
the privacy of their superiors, transact such business not in the Castle, but
in one of the village inns. Except for select village women, who become
mistresses to the Castellans, townsfolk as a rule may not enter the Castle
unless they are actually employed there. Finally, with all the authority
vested in the lordly officials, there is still someone above them, Count
Westwest, whose name is scarcely mentioned in the novel but whose
significance staggers the imagination. If the officials are inaccessible, the
Count is inconceivable, as if he were some sacrosanct entity residing, as his
name suggests, beyond the setting sun.

We can imagine the immensity of the Count's stature by comparing
him with Klamm, whose title is only "Chief of Department X." Klamm
is a tangible presence in the novel. Though his subordinates make every
effort to shield him from public view, people have (or claim to have) seen
him. He regularly visits one of the village inns, locking himself up in his
private room; he eats, drinks, works hard, and has had many mistresses.
Descriptions of him vary, but if we can believe that it is Klamm whom K.
sees through the keyhole of Klamm's room in the inn, then he is a stout
man with a beard who generally dozes off in the evening after his dinner
and beer. Thus Klamm is human enough. At the same time, he is scarcely
less of a god-figure than the Count. Even if most people have never seen
him, they are aware of his influence in the smallest detail of their lives and
they are devoted to him. The mere utterance of his name, if one dare make
it in public, immediately evokes a reverential silence. Former mistresses feel
transfigured by him, as Leda was by the swan (Frieda begins to lose her
beauty after leaving Klamm). He is characterized as an eagle, whose salient
qualities are actually congruent with those ascribed to the Castle:

[10] Franz Kafka, *The Castle,* tr. Willa and Edwin Muir, New York, 1968. Subsequent quotations from *The Castle* are from this edition.

> Once the landlady had compared Klamm to an eagle, and that had
> seemed absurd in K.'s eyes, but it did not seem absurd now; he
> thought of Klamm's remoteness, of his impregnable dwelling, of his
> silence, broken perhaps only by cries such as K. had never yet heard, of
> his downward-pressing gaze, which could never be proved or
> disproved, of his wheelings, which could never be disturbed by
> anything that K. did down below, which far above he followed at the
> behest of incomprehensible laws and which only for instants were
> visible—all these things Klamm and the eagle had in common.

K.'s realization of the subtle power of the Castle, and of Klamm in
particular, comes only after a series of demoralizing experiences. He arrives
with certain claims upon the authorities, but he is soon made to realize his
utter insignificance. The Castle scarcely makes a move, yet almost
immediately K. finds himself entangled in a hopeless maze. The Mayor,
Klamm's deputy in the town, flatly denies that any wrong has been done to
K.; however, to compensate K. for the inconvenience he has been put to,
the Mayor offers him the demeaning job of school janitor! K. seeks redress
directly from the Castle, but he is informed in no uncertain terms that he
may never visit it. He tries to see Klamm when the latter comes to the
village, but seemingly everyone acts to prevent him. He is assigned a
messenger, Barnabas, to act as liason between him and Klamm, but he can
never be certain whether the messages will be delivered or whether their
delivery will be so delayed that they are worthless when they are received.
He does receive two letters from Klamm (at least they bear his signature);
but their contents are so bizarre as to suggest that either Klamm is totally
out of touch with K.'s case or is simply amusing himself with him. K. is
also assigned two utterly worthless assistants, who only pester and en-
cumber him and who are actually taking orders from somebody else. Even
his fiance Frieda, formerly Klamm's mistress, tries to keep him from
Klamm (as Kafka's mother attempted to forestall any confrontation
between him and his father), and when K. persists she runs off with one of
his assistants. Castellans and townsfolk alike appear either indifferent or
openly hostile to him; the few who offer friendship are suspect. And K. is
soon oppressed with the feeling that he is the victim of an insidious
conspiracy, originating in the Castle yet enlisting the entire village.
     But it would be uncharacteristic of Kafka to leave us with so simple an
explanation of K.'s misfortunes. The same facts can be interpreted so as to
cast more blame on him. Naturally, K. is an outsider, but he himself

prolongs his alienation. The Castle offers him free meals and lodgings; he is also assured that the job aş janitor is only a temporary expediency. The Castle will also permit him to marry the girl whom he has seduced from Klamm, who is after all the very embodiment of the Castle. K. accepts the job and agrees to marry Frieda. But these intentions are halfhearted, for he suspects that placid adaptation to village life will only make him indistinguishable from everybody else and thus encourage the authorities to ignore his singular aim of inhabiting the Castle:

> If K. was willing to become a workman he could do so, but he would
> have to do it in grim earnest, without any other prospect.

Thus he discharges his janitorial duties perfunctorily; despite Frieda's pleadings he is forever running off for news from the Castle and leaving her with the enigmatic assistants. He becomes, temporarily, an iconoclast scorning decorum and challenging ancient ritual. He refuses to cooperate with minor officials or offers his cooperation only on condition that it will guarantee him a meeting with Klamm. He outrageously tries to waylay Klamm in a village inn. Behind the bar of the same inn he seduces Frieda and induces her to live with him (possibly out of a genuine attraction to her, but also out of an awareness that she has lain in the arms of the powerful Klamm); and we have good reason to suspect that he hopes to use her as a pawn in negotiations with that dignitary.

K. is aware that Klamm has no desire to see him, that thrusting himself on him will hardly endear K. to him, and that even if he were granted an interview he would not know what to say to Klamm. But his determination to penetrate the Castle becomes an irrational passion. He resolves that

> ... he, K., he only and no one else, should attain to Klamm, and
> should attain to him not to rest with him, but to go on beyond him,
> farther yet, into the Castle.

Typical of Kafka's obsessed characters, he will sacrifice everything to his end: the home he left beyond the mountains (he rejects out of hand Frieda's suggestion that they leave the village) or the home that he can have with Frieda in the village. He is prepared to accept any hardship at first, because

> ... that sort of thing could be put up with, it belonged to the
> ordinary continual petty annoyances of life, it was nothing compared

with what K. was striving for, and he had not come here simply to
lead an honored and comfortable life.

In this interpretation of the facts, then, it is K.'s fanaticism (certainly no
less than the indifference of the Castle and villagers) which isolates him.
Paradoxically, he demands acceptance into a system which precludes his
right to demand. This predicament is dramatically scored when K. posts
himself outside the hotel in which Klamm is staying, determined to
confront that gentleman when he comes out. In order to shield Klamm
from K., a subofficial attempts to persuade K. to leave. K. refuses; and after
he stands guard in the cold and empty courtyard for what seems like hours,
the lights in the inn are suddenly turned off, signalling that Klamm will
spend the night there rather than expose himself to K. K. feels that he has
won a point, but like Underground Man at Zverkov's farewell party, he
knows too that his victory is a dubious one:

> . . . it seemed to K. as if at last those people had broken off all relations
> with him, and as if now in reality he were freer than he had ever been,
> and at liberty to wait here in this place, usually forbidden to him, as
> long as he desired, and had won a freedom such as hardly anybody else
> had ever succeeded in winning, and as if nobody could dare to touch
> him or drive him away, or even speak to him; but—this conviction
> was at least equally strong—as if at the same time there was nothing
> more senseless, nothing more hopeless, than this freedom, this wait-
> ing, this inviolability.

The more K. insists on his rights, the less they are honored. When he
reminds the Mayor that he has been summoned to a job that does not exist,
the Mayor replies that although an "error has occurred," it is only a "trifling
miscalculation" because K.'s case is "one of the least important among the
least important" whereas in "great matters" the Castle never makes an
error! On the surface, the Mayor seems to be uttering pure nonsense. In
effect, however, he is saying that K. is too insignificant for the Castle to
admit that it has erred where he is concerned: it can only injure K. as one
casually (and probably unintentionally) steps on a bug which happens to
crawl under his foot. Furthermore, the Castle is a closed, self-contained
system which, through its Control Authority, is programmed to catch
slight (or in the Mayor's words, "so-called") errors, such as in K.'s case;
therefore, with the rigor of a bank audit, it balances everything out in the

end, canceling its error merely by acknowledging it. For K., who refuses to be a mere cipher in the Castle's ledgers, the mistake is real enough (he construes the Castle's offer of the janitor's job as acknowledgment of its initial error). Convinced that he is a victim of arbitrary power, he bemoans the "ludicrous bungling that in certain circumstances may decide the life of a human being." But no one heeds him.

In the dialogue between K. and the Mayor, Kafka presents two opposing positions, and the reader's sympathy shifts to whoever is speaking at the moment. But for all the clues he gives us, it is impossible to blame unequivocally either K. or the Castle for K.'s misfortunes. The Castle is simply what it is: it is beyond human judgment. Yet K. suffers through its mistake, though admittedly he compounds his suffering through subsequent actions of his own. We may ally ourselves with a godless Voltaire, who points gleefully at the Lisbon earthquake; or we may agree with a Leibnitz, who insists that since there is only one "possible" world it must be the "best." Nonetheless, whether our sympathies are with the Castle or with K., they can only be subjective; for Kafka scrupulously conceals his own final judgment in the ageless strife between man and Providence, if indeed he ever made one.

Kafka is deliberately ambiguous in the novel (mention has already been made of the literal darkness in *The Castle*); specks of light appear momentarily, but instead of lighting K.'s way they lead him into profounder obscurity. Familiar objects assume unfamiliar relationships or take on a totally new aspect from moment to moment, as in a dream. For example, K.'s messenger to the Castle loses his shining glamor once he is off duty; K.'s assistant Jeremiah, docile, playful and somewhat simpleminded while in K.'s service, suddenly becomes hard, shrewd and apparently many years older the moment K. dismisses him; the peasants, ordinarily simple and gentle, turn without warning into grotesque masses of flesh or pure, raw energy that can instantly destroy anything that stands in their way. The world of *The Castle* is commonplace enough, but it is punctured with harsh, surrealistic touches, the uncanny meanings of which K. can surely feel but never quite understand.

Yet there are no Gothic trapdoors or supernatural paraphernalia in the novel. On the contrary, the reader is overwhelmed with rational explanations for what appears to be incredible. Character after character proves to be an expert, hairsplitting dialectician. At the same time, definitive conclusions are impossible because what one disputant presents as absolute

fact another reduces to a shaky hypothesis, offering a substitute explanation that is equally vulnerable. Even if we could trust K.'s objectivity, he
is handicapped by the fact that he receives information in pieces, from
diverse and apparently contradictory sources (as does a detective stymied in
the initial stages of his investigation); and K., as we have seen, has his own
prejudices, such as underestimating the Castle throughout the early part of
the novel. Possibly the Castle can clear everything up, but it chooses to be
silent. On the other hand, the Castle may be fraudulent or self-deluding,
having succeeded in humbugging the villagers. But this we cannot know
either because none of the characters (at least none of the ones who talk
about the Castle) can comprehend it in its entirety. To an omniscient
observer—say the author Kafka—the apparently mysterious and absurd
world of the novel may be perfectly clear and logical. But Kafka does not
provide us with such an all-knowing point of view (his fiction is invariably
told through a *limited* narrative point of view). Consequently, individual
characters (and readers) tend to believe only what they are predisposed to
believe and not just what is incontestably borne out by the facts.

Kafka, then, deliberately curtails the reader's comprehension in order to
discourage moral judgment. We have no objective basis for labeling the
Castle "benign" or "fiendish" or even "indifferent," though it may appear
to be so. We can ultimately only speculate about its workings, and then
primarily because of people's reactions to it rather than overt actions of its
own (actually, the Castle seems to "do" very little in the novel). When, for
example, Barnabas' sister angrily turns down an invitation to become the
mistress of an important official, she and her family are immediately
ostracized by the rest of the village. The family naturally assumes that it is
being punished by the Castle, either directly or indirectly. But when
Barnabas' father appeals to the Castle for forgiveness, the latter informs
him that there is nothing to forgive—no ostensible crime has been committed:

> Yet before he could be forgiven he had to prove his guilt, which was
> denied in all the departments.

Thus the family's guilt transcends the initial incident that triggered it off,
just as Franz Kafka's "boundless" guilt persisted long after he had forgotten the childhood experiences that had precipitated it. Like Kafka in
tortured preoccupation with his father, the obsessed family is its own worst

enemy. The Castle has done it no harm (none, at least, that anyone knows of); yet long after the other villagers have forgotten the incident and the family's material fortunes have modestly improved, it continues to torment itself with its unfounded guilt.

K., too, makes frenetic appeals to the inscrutable Castle, whose true nature he only takes for granted; and it is more than coincidence that he should ally himself with Barnabas' family and even contemplate living with them when all other doors are closed to him. But because Kafka never completed the novel, there is doubt as to how far he meant to push the analogy between K. and that luckless family. If he intended to have K. die of exhaustion in his assaults on the Castle, then the similarity is complete. That K. does eventually begin to give in to fatigue seems unquestionable. Though his weariness is already apparent in the first chapter, it is climaxed in the third chapter from the end. Here he has reached the point where his only desire is to sleep. In a particular scene from this chapter he literally falls asleep as one of the Castle Secretaries (the first to be friendly to him) actually offers to help him to enter the Castle. The offer may be bogus, the Secretary may simply be teasing K. Kafka, characteristically, provides us no basis for determining the functionary's sincerity. What is certain, however, is that K. up to this point would normally have leaped at such an offer and would have been prepared to pin all his hopes on it.

Possibly, K. here may be so physically exhausted that nothing could keep him from falling asleep. On the other hand, he might simply be permitting himself to fall asleep because he attaches no significance to the Secretary's offer. Much has happened to K. since his arrival. He has been humiliated, frustrated, physically assaulted, and possibly deceived. He has every reason to be skeptical of the boon voluntarily proffered him by a total stranger who belongs to the heretofore unfriendly Castle. In this and the remaining two chapters of the novel K.'s chief concerns appear to be food and lodging. If only for the sake of survival, he moves closer to the villagers, two of whom suddenly invite him to live with them. We begin to discern a reversal in his overall attitude, particularly in the last chapter. He has mellowed. He now seems less aggressive and strident, more resigned to the impossibility of his quest and more receptive to other options. He also seems to have acquired some of Franz Kafka's humility. Significantly, he reproaches himself for his brashness and seems to have acquired the villagers' simple respect for Klamm and the Castle. His new humility reveals itself most clearly in his attempt to console Pepi, who has unsuc-

cessfully attempted to supplant Frieda as barmaid at the prestigious
Herrenhof and as Klamm's favorite. Seeing in Pepi's anxious striving a
similitude for himself and Barnabas' family, he tells her:

> I don't know whether it is like this, and my own guilt is by no means
> clear to me; only, when I compare myself with you something of this
> kind dawns on me: it is as if we had both striven too intensely, too
> noisily, too childishly, with too little experience, to get something
> that for instance with Frieda's calm and Frieda's matter-of-factness
> can be got easily and without much ado. We have tried to get it by
> crying, by scratching, by tugging—just as a child tugs at the
> tablecloth, gaining nothing, but only bringing all the splendid
> things down on the floor and putting them out of its reach forever.

The mood here is one of resignation. It is hardly consistent with the
assumed ending of the novel, in which K. would supposedly have died of
sheer exhaustion in his attempts to reach the Castle. After all, Kafka only
told Max Brod that he might complete the novel in this manner, he never
actually wrote a conclusion; and (given his meticulousness as a writer) he
might well have written a totally different one from the presumed one if he
had lived long enough to think his subject through to his complete
satisfaction. It is also possible that he might never have decided on any
definitive ending (at least one that found its way into print), because K.'s
ambivalent reactions to the Castle reflect Kafka's own unresolved conflicts
with absolute authority.

But it is not necessary to conjecture about a finale which was never
written. From what Kafka did complete, we can still draw the unassailable
conclusion that one either accepts the Castle on its own terms or destroys
himself defying it. Certainly throughout most of the novel K. has been a
nonconformist, but there is nothing of Byron's heroics to his recalcitrance,
nor does he experience the "absurd" delight in revolt that Camus' Rebel
does. At its best, K.'s revolt is a Faustian obsession to scale the Castle
heights which are out-of-bounds to him; at its worst, it is the petulance of
a frustrated child. And it is always equivocal. For example, on his first night
in town, still self-confident, he seduces Frieda keenly aware that his
benefactor Klamm sits in a room only a few feet away. When moments
later the unpredictable Frieda shouts to Klamm that she is leaving him for
K., K.'s self-assurance gives way to *angst*. In a moment of wild despair, he

. . . started up, and on his knees beside Frieda gazed round him in the uncertain light of dawn. What had happened? Where were his hopes? What could he expect from Frieda now that she had betrayed everything? Instead of feeling his way with prudence befitting the greatness of his enemy and of his ambition, he had spent a whole night wallowing in puddles of beer, the smell of which was nearly overpowering.

K.'s forwardness (which some of the villagers secretly admire) is often only bravado. He knows that he has limitations, but he is uncertain as to what they are. Like a child who tests his parents (the child Franz Kafka, whimpering moments before the father puts him out on the porch), K. continually tries the patience of the Castle. Of course, what he really wants from it is acceptance. But when the Castle withholds overt signs of love, at least the ones that K. can read, he invites its displeasure. That, at least, is preferable to its intolerable indifference.

On the other hand, we cannot necessarily conclude that Kafka advocates simple conformity in *The Castle*. If K. does submit in the end, his submission is still distinct from the doglike devotion of the villagers, of whom he says, "Fear of the authorities is born in you here." To the faithful townsfolk, the Castle is beyond criticism, despite its aristocratic distance from them, the rudeness of its officials (who exercize the *droit du seigneur* in their cavalier treatment of the town's women), its arbitrariness, its unpredictability, its absolute power over them. Obedient, stolid and uncomplaining, in agreement with the under-Castellan who proclaims that "the village belongs to the Castle," they see no opposition between themselves and the Castle and, therefore, do not feel the sting of its authority. But K. will always be conscious of his subjugation. Like Kafka, he will suffer from underground man's sense of impotence. He will yearn for knowledge that is withheld from him, remain sensitive to affronts that are heaped upon him, and cherish recognition of an individuality that is only scorned. And, if only to himself, he will continue to ascribe at least some of his discontent to a force beyond him, castigating what he freely acknowledges to be the object of his deepest longings. If he does slip quietly into anonymity, it will not be because he is convinced his plaints are unfounded, but only because they are useless.

Thus Kafka neither praises nor condemns conformity. He only demonstrates in the novel, as he did in his unhappy life, that it is necessary

for survival. And Kafka did choose to survive. Like the character in his
"The Hunger Artist," Kafka found the "food" of life distasteful and did
contemplate suicide. Yet he was incapable of such an act. Possibly, he had
too much of Hesse's moral revulsion for it; or he may simply have felt that
one dies soon enough ("Like a dog," cries Joseph K. in *The Trial*, who
nevertheless refuses to execute himself and thus spare his executioners the
job). Whatever his reasons, Kafka dissociated himself from the suicide:

> The suicide is the prisoner who sees the gallows being erected in the
> prison yard, mistakenly thinks it is the one intended for him, breaks
> out of his cell in the night, and goes down and hangs himself.
> ("Notebooks," p. 99)

Kafka rejected the noose for underground, his spiritual prison, where he
waited in vain for a Castle or a Law or a forgiving Father to release him.

Chapter 3

Hermann Hesse: *Steppenwolf*

Foreseeing in Underground Man the breakdown of Western civilization, Dostoevsky urged a return to traditional faith. Hesse, on the other hand, welcomed the new rebel. In his study of Dostoevsky, *In Sight of Chaos* (1920), Hesse interpreted Dostoevsky's unruly iconoclasts as simply challenging modes and values in the West that were beyond salvaging. By 1920 the cultural chaos that Dostoevsky had predicted was already a reality.

Hesse's protagonists, at least in his later novels, do not totally despair, as Underground Man does. If they are rebels, they are also knights-errant in modern dress seeking an ideal that will rejuvenate themselves and their lackluster times; and being capable of love, faith and commitment, they manage to achieve a measure of fulfillment unknown to Underground Man. For example, Siddhartha, in the novel by that name, realizes nirvana after rejecting traditional Hinduism and Buddhism; Goldmund in *Narcissus and Goldmund* experiences religious bliss after repeatedly violating the moral strictures of the Church. Yet Hesse is no optimist doling out platitudes. His heroes suffer, like the battered Goldmund dying from a beating administered him in a ditch or Siddhartha on the verge of a nervous breakdown. Like Underground Man they doubt and punish themselves; they tend to be cynical about the world; and they contemplate suicide. Indeed, Harry Haller, in the first half of *Steppenwolf,* is literally an underground man.

Once an eminent writer, the head of a family, and the center of a circle of admiring friends, Harry is now an idle, forty-eight year old hermit. He spends much of the day in bed. At night he sometimes reads, but increasingly he prowls the streets or paces his room like a caged beast. His room is always littered with innumerable books scattered around in

disarray, empty wine bottles, cigar ashes, and tidbits of food intended for
meals which he has neglected to eat. He might go for days without
addressing a word to anyone but shopkeepers and waitresses. He is also
ailing physically, suffering from sciatica and gout, the pain of which is
often so acute that he must take laudanum to assuage it. His condition is
aggravated by his heavy drinking, and it is not always certain whether the
matinal pain between his eyes signals an attack of neuralgia or is simply a
hangover.

Having come to maturity at the turn of the century, and having lived
through the devastation of World War I, he has witnessed the dissolution
of the traditions and certitudes of his childhood. Harry's underground is
the nightmarish postwar wasteland, with its overcrowded railroad stations,
hotels and cafes; its oppressive jazz music, variety entertainments, and
world exhibitions; its reactionary and jingoistic press; its automobiles and
technology; its corruption in politics and finance; its frenzied pace; its
hunger for the novel and the bizarre; its vulgarity. Since his attachments
are to a bygone era, Harry, like Underground Man, cannot affirm the
standards and styles of the immediate world around him. Hence, he sees
himself as a lonely "Steppenwolf," a stray wolf from the remote steppes of
Russia:

> I stood outside all social circles, alone, beloved by none, mistrusted by
> many, in unceasing and bitter conflict with public opinion and
> morality; and though I lived in a bourgeois setting, I was all the same
> an utter stranger to this world in all I thought and felt. Religion,
> country, family, state, all lost their value and meant nothing to me
> any more. The pomposity of the sciences, societies, and arts disgusted
> me.[1]

But if Harry is critical of the times, he also shares Underground Man's
self-disgust. No one is more keenly aware, and less forgiving, of the
shambles he has made of his life:

> Everything was old, withered, grey, limp and spent, and stank of
> staleness and decay. Dear God, how was it possible? How had I, with
> the wings of youth and poetry, come to this! Art and travel and the
> glow of ideals—and now this!

---

[1] Hermann Hesse, *Steppenwolf,* tr. Basil Creighton, New York, 1963. Subsequent quotations from *Steppenwolf* are from this edition.

But the voice here only echoes conventional values. Even were Harry to return to his earlier way of life he would be subjected to mockery from another source within him, his "wolf." Harry, the Steppenwolf, conceives of himself as a dual personality, consisting of "wolf" and "man." The man, according to Harry, is the civilized, rational part of himself, while the wolf represents his dark, instinctual nature. But he has so exaggerated their differences—the man is godlike, the wolf is lowly and despicable—that they admit of no synthesis or compromise. So if Harry has a beautiful thought or expresses a noble sentiment or does a kindly deed, the wolf grins at him in contempt; if he loses his temper or yields to the promptings of the flesh, the overcivilized man punishes him. It is therefore impossible for him to enjoy the pleasures of either his spiritual or his animal nature without an immediate reaction of guilt. Occasionally, wolf and man abide in relative harmony within the Steppenwolf, and he experiences a welcome, if lukewarm, tranquility. More and more, however, they are at enmity with one another.

Harry, then, is torn by conflicts both within himself and with the society around him. Yet there is an even deeper cause for discontent in him. This is man himself—not the individual Harry, but the human condition. The Steppenwolf has Underground Man's yearning for a state of being that transcends imperfect man as we know him. He envisions the realm of the "Immortals," those superior beings, usually artists and thinkers, whose lives or work stand as monuments to the human spirit. Though Harry has a clearer notion of his ideal than Underground Man has of his, he too can only suggest it. The Immortals dwell in

> . . . timeless space, enraptured, re-fashioned and immersed in a crys-
> talline eternity like ether, and the cool starry brightness and radiant
> serenity of this world outside the earth. . . .

Ageless, sexless, beyond all care, they are capable of the "eternal, divine laughter," which can only astound and befuddle the humorless Steppenwolf every time he has a visitation from them.

Whether this world is to be taken as real or merely symbolic of a potentiality in humans, for Harry it has profound significance. Indeed, it would be no exaggeration to say that he lives only for his intermittent glimpses into it, which come to him without warning when he reads a passage from one of his Immortal poets or hears a certain bar of music or, on occasion, when he takes his first glass of wine for the day! And always, he is so overwhelmed by the experience that he can only describe it in figurative language:

> ... the door was opened of a sudden to the other world. I sped
> through heaven and saw God at work. I suffered holy pains. I dropped
> all my defenses and was afraid of nothing in the world.

But now, as a middle-aged man, he rarely has visitations from the other world; he is blinded by the "dirt" and "dust" of this world. Life, then, is either heaven or hell for Harry, but mostly hell.

Harry's defenses will no longer do. Relief must come through something new and overpowering, something perhaps "magical." And this is precisely what does happen. One night Harry stumbles past an old church door on which dancing lights announce an invitation to the "Magic Theatre" (the revelation of which is postponed to the last section of the novel). That same evening, in the same place, a mysterious passerby hands him a "Treatise on the Steppenwolf." The Treatise, written specifically for Harry (Hesse never tells us who its author is), is a lengthy analysis of Harry and his problems; it describes, abstractly and theoretically, the difficult way out of underground. Harry's teacher in the next phase of the novel will be the enigmatic Hermine, with whose help he will actually begin the painful metamorphosis prescribed by the Treatise. In the last section of the book, the Magic Theatre, the extraordinary Pablo will replace Hermine as Harry's guru; he will reinforce what little progress Harry has made under Hermine's tutelage.

Diverting Harry's gaze from the evils of society to the distortions in his own mind, the Treatise attacks several of his cherished beliefs. One is his very notion of the Steppenwolf, which the Treatise characterizes as a gross oversimplification. It takes Harry to task for his equation of the wolf with nature and the man with spirit, because this distinction erroneously relegates to the wolf (and hence nature) what is mean and regressive and ascribes to the man, or "spirit," only the loftiest of human attributes, that is to say, the condition not of humans but of the Immortals:

> He assigns, we fear, whole provinces of his soul to the "man" which
> are a long way from being human, and parts of his being to the wolf
> that long ago have left the wolf behind.

The Treatise points out that although Nature (the primal Mother) and

Spirit (God the Father) exist separately as transcendent metaphysical entities, in man they are inseparable; and that Harry would be hard put to disentangle one from the other in any of his actions, thoughts or feelings. Indeed, even a wolf has "spiritual" experiences such as love, tenderness and suffering. Moreover, by depreciating what is "wolfish" in him Harry discredits what are, as often as not, his richest treasures.

Thus, the Treatise persists, he suffers not because two selves are too many in one man but because they are too few! The distinction between wolf and man is analogous to classifying a bower of different flowers according to whether they are edible or inedible and ignoring such qualities as color, texture, form and fragrance. Man, as he is conceived of in the Treatise, is complex and multifaceted. He consists of a "bundle of selves"; his soul is a "manifold world, a constellated heaven, a chaos of forms, of states and stages, of inheritances and potentialities," all of them containing the admixture of nature and spirit. Man, the Treatise insists, is continually evolving; and if Harry is to break out of the prison of his own creation, he must tap the buried selves within him.

The Treatise cites another significant blind spot in Harry's thinking, namely, how he sees himself in relation to society (in Hesse's novel, the middle class, or bourgeoisie). His ignorance of his real connection with the bourgeois results both from his incomplete knowledge of himself and from a basic misconception of the bourgeoisie, at which he has so often railed while living in its midst. The Treatise defines the bourgeois as follows:

> Now what we call the "bourgeois," when regarded as an element always to be found in human life, is nothing else than the search for a balance.... [The bourgeois] will never surrender himself either to lust or to asceticism. He will never become a martyr or agree to his own destruction. On the contrary, his ideal is not to give up but to maintain his own identity. He strives neither for the saintly nor its opposite. The absolute is his abhorrence. He may be ready to serve God, but not by giving up the fleshpots. He is ready to be virtuous, but likes to be easy and comfortable in this world as well.... The bourgeois is consequently by nature a creature of weak impulses, anxious, fearful of giving himself away and easy to rule. Therefore, he has substituted majority for power, law for force, and the polling booth for responsibility.

The Treatise is not concerned with the values of the saint and sinner, which are in opposition, but with the styles in which each realizes these values, which are identical. Both have the capacity for total surrender, the one to the body (nature) and the other to the spirit. They live short, tragic lives. But in their freedom from compromise and hesitation, in their capacity to let go, they are closer to the Absolute, the Immortals, than is the bourgeois. The bourgeois, says the Treatise, attempts to cheat both the Father (spirit) and the Mother (nature) by taking from both what will ensure him a comfortable and secure, if flaccid, existence:

> "Man," whatever people think of him, is never anything more than a temporary bourgeois compromise. Convention rejects and bans certain of the more naked instincts, a little consciousness, morality and debestialization is called for, and a modicum of spirit is not only permitted but even thought necessary.

Harry does aspire to saintliness in those moments when the "man" in him is the dominant force; conversely, he yearns for the dark, wild world of the sinner when the "wolf" in him is the master. But these are only halfhearted, ambivalent gropings. Harry never reaches either extreme—what the Treatise calls the "unconditioned" life; for he clings too desperately to life, despite his dubious contemplation of suicide. He is, in fact, a bourgeois, who until now has refused to acknowledge his kinship with the bourgeoisie. Doubtless, he is an unerring critic of modern society. Yet there is something of the pose in his rebellion. In many respects, he is the favored child of the bourgeoisie. He lodges in comfortable, well-scrubbed houses, though he looks down upon the cultural attainments of his landlords. He wears expensive clothes, yet damns the fashion magazines. He travels widely, but always as a romantic suffering from homesickness. He lives on annuities, while excoriating the evils of capitalism.

But Harry is not a typical bourgeois. More sensitive, imaginative and conscious, he differs from the latter in the "higher development of his individuality." He at least is able to see into the sickness of the times and knows that he himself is not well (although he cannot as yet isolate his symptoms). If he shakes his fist at the bourgeoisie and lives on the fringe of society, it is because he is aware of another world, the starry realm of the Immortals. Underground Steppenwolf is alienated from society, and for good reason. But he is not free of it.

Having exposed Harry's confusion about himself, the Treatise challenges what is perhaps his last comfort, suicide. Like other underground men who are driven by anxiety and self-doubt, he feels that his ego is an extremely "dangerous, dubious and doomed germ of nature" which will instantly disintegrate at the slightest shock. And he is convinced that in all probability he will be the cause of his own death. At the same time, he sees in death a deliverance from the torments of this world and a return to God the Father, to Nature the Womb, or to the Valhalla of the Immortals—". . . into the All," as Hesse puts it. Hence, he has set his fiftieth birthday as the probable day of his suicide if by that time his suffering has not abated. But the omniscient author of the Treatise shrewdly divines that, deep down, Harry does not wish to give up his life. Aware of another world, he is fundamentally a religious man, for whom suicide is reprehensible. Moreover, a stubborn if buried pride in Harry resists it as an ignominious defeat. Thus on the day he has appointed for his suicide, the horrified Steppenwolf finds that he is incapable of the deed.

It is this submerged instinct for life that the Treatise attempts to arouse in Hesse's despairing intellectual. The Treatise flatly rejects suicide as a way to God:

> From the very start there is no innocence and no singleness. Every created thing, even the simplest, is already guilty, already multiple. It has been thrown into the muddy stream of being and may never more swim back again to its source. . . . Nor will suicide really solve your problem, unhappy Steppenwolf. You will, instead, embark on the longer and wearier and harder road of life. You will have to multiply many times your two-fold being and complicate your complexities still further. . . . All births mean separation from the All, the confinement within limitation, the separation from God, the pangs of being born ever anew. The return into the All, the dissolution of painful individuation, the reunion with God means the expansion of the soul until it is able once more to embrace the All.

*   *   *

This passage is, in effect, Hesse's personal reinterpretation of Hinduism and Buddhism. Like the Treatise, both of these philosophies postulate a single, timeless essence (Brahma, the Buddha-nature), of which the visible world, including human life, is only a passing manifestation. Brahma is our essence; therefore, we can never literally be separated from Brahma. However, at birth we assume a human body and a human consciousness (as distinguished from the Superconsciousness of Brahma). We then become aware of time, distance, change, finiteness, individuality; and consequently we *experience* separation from Brahma even though in essence we *are* Brahma.

To be born is to be thrown into the ocean of life (the Hindu-Buddhist *samsara,* Hesse's *nature*). But our destiny is to return to our divine origin (the Hindu-Buddhist *nirvana,* Hesse's "re-union with God"): having been born "already guilty, already multiple," we seek a return to our pristine innocence and unity with the All. In other words, the purpose of human life is to compensate for the imperfections that began with our birth! And if necessary, this compensation (*karma*) may require several lifetimes. Thus human life describes a circle, with each reincarnation constituting a point on its circumference and karma determining the rate at which we travel it.

The Hindus and Gautama Buddha developed a precise method for achieving enlightenment and escaping the Wheel of Life. It involved *meditation*–penetrating through the successive veils of mundane consciousness to Superconsciousness and the divine Self; exemplary moral conduct, with good and evil being clearly defined; and a renunciation of this world, the initial cause of our divorce from the Absolute.

But for Hesse, Hinduism and the teachings of Gautama, like Christianity, are too constrictive. He can accept meditation, which leads to the "expansion of the soul." But he rejects the Hindu's and Buddhist's rigid morality, as well as their denigration of this world. Hence, Hesse is inclined more toward their indirect offshoot, Zen Buddhism, and to Chinese Taoism.[2] In common with these latter philosophies, Hesse sees "good" and "evil," and all other opposites (night and day, life and death, male and female, wolf and man) as only relative. They are abstractions which men, in an imperfect state of awareness, construct from surface manifestations of the single essence (Tao, the Buddha-nature, the spirit of the Immortals). According to Taoist Lao Tzu:

> For is and is-not come together;
> Hard and easy are complementary;
> Long and short are relative;

[2] Zen (in Chinese, *Ch'an*) is a development of the Indian Mahayana Buddhism after it was transplanted in China and Japan. It is also largely conditioned by Taoism, the mystic rival to the formalistic teachings of Confucius in China several centuries before the birth of Christ. Since our concern is with the influence of Zen and Taoism on Hesse, I am making mention only of their similarities, which are considerable. The reader, however, should not lose sight of the fact that they are two separate philosophies.

> High and low are comparative;
> Pitch and sound make harmony;
> Before and after are a sequence.[3]

And the Zen poet Seng Ts'an admonishes, "Do not like, do not dislike; all will then be clear./ Make a hairbreadth difference, and Heaven and Earth are set apart."[4] Thus we must, in the spirit of the Gnostic, banish judgment and acknowledge all things, including our dark nature (Harry's wolf), for they are all manifestations of the divine. And contrary to the ascetic Hindu *samana* and the monastic Gautama (or the Harry who retreats to his study), the Treatise advocates the Zen and Taoistic practice of involvement in the world. The infinite is in the finite: in the stone, the river, and the stock exchange! Again, Seng Ts'an warns us, "If you want to follow the doctrine of the One, do not rage against the World of the Senses./ Only by accepting the World of the Senses can you share in the True Perception."[5] The Hindu nirvana, the state of beatitude beyond the individual's last reincarnation, is replaced by *satori*—the flash of total, exhilirating awareness which the enlightened devotee can experience in the here and now—which, indeed, comes even to Steppenwolf on those rare occasions when his Immortals reveal themselves to him. And the moral law of karma, along with our literal reincarnations for the imperfections of past existences, becomes the dynamic principle of change in this lifetime, according to which we blunder and suffer and postpone satori.

Reunion with the Immortals, then, is possible for Harry only through growth and knowledge, the piling of experience upon experience, the recognition and liberation of the undiscovered Harrys in his own mind, the willingness to accept the absurdities of this world along with the

---

[3] *Tao Tê Ching,* tr. R. B. Blakney, New York, 1955, p. 54. (This edition is A Mentor Religious Classic published under the title, *The Way of Life.* Subsequent quotations from *Tao Tê Ching* are from this edition.) I shall refer to Lao Tzu as the author of this book, even though his authorship is questionable.

[4] Seng Ts'an, quoted in E. A. Burtt, *The Teachings of the Compassionate Buddha,* New York, 1955, p. 227. (A Mentor Religious Classic.) Originally published by The Philosophical Library (New York) in Edward Conze, et al., eds., *Buddhist Texts Through the Ages* (as "Seng Ts'an's Poem on Trust in the Heart"), pp. 295-298.

[5] In the novel *Siddhartha* Hesse's hero, having renounced the teachings of his Brahmin forebears, must hurl himself into commerce and sensuality before he can achieve the serenity that transcends them. Goldmund, in *Narcissus and Goldmund,* must exhaust the offerings of the senses before he can experience his beatitude.

sublime visitations from the other—in short, living and more living, until
his soul expands to God's own dimensions. To live in the society he scorns
Harry must develop the fundamental Zen attitude of humor, which the
Treatise describes as the ability to

> ... live in the world as though it were not the world, to respect the
> law and yet to stand above it, to have possessions as though "one
> possessed nothing," to renounce as though it were no renuncia-
> tion. ...

We literally live in this world—for mortals there is nowhere else! But we
are "beyond" it when we avoid attachment to the particulars that constitute it, and when we resonate instead with the pattern behind all quotidian
reality. Life is like the river in *Siddhartha,* and either we flow with it or
smash up on the shoals of our own intractability.[6] All humor presupposes
incongruity and imbalance (for example the pompous dignitary slips and
falls on a banana peel). To grasp incongruity we must have a notion of the
total structure from which the absurd part has deviated: it is the simul-
taneous intuition of the two that evokes our laughter. Of course, humor
need not simply be laughter at the grotesque. It can also be a paean of
thanksgiving for the beauty, harmony and splendor of the universe. The
clownish monks, Han-shen and Shih-te, the corpulent folk-god Pu-Tai and
other good-humored fellows in Zen art are gleeful because, in their
enlightenment, not only do they see into human foibles (including their
own), but they are also moment-by-moment witnesses to nature's celebration of life. The Immortals of *Steppenwolf* laugh their icy laugh; with
Hesse's other favored characters—Vasudeva and Siddhartha in *Siddhartha,*
Leo in *The Journey to the East,* the Magister Musicae in *The Glass Bead
Game*—the laughter gives way to a gentle smile, and the rollicking humor
to an almost otherworldly serenity.

Actually, humor in any form for Hesse is consciousness, maximum
consciousness pushed to the vision of the mystic. It is the ability to bring
"every aspect of human existence within the rays of its prism" and not to be

[6]"Alive, a man is supple, soft;
In death, unbending, rigorous.
All creatures, grass and trees, alive
Are plastic but are pliant too,
And dead, are friable and dry."
                                        (*Tao Tê Ching,* p. 129)

deluded into identifying any part with the whole. (The enlightened figures in Zen paintings are often depicted with large, bulging eyes, as if they could see out of the sides of their heads and could take in the entire universe with a couple of quick glances.) To be sure, Harry sees more than the bourgeois does, but his heightened consciousness, like Underground Man's, only causes him more suffering. If he could enlarge his awareness still further, if he could gaze through the surface strife and contradictions—beneath wolf and man, saint and bourgeois—he might be able to grasp the essential unity that embraces all of these dichotomies. And, in the spirit of Lao Tzu's Wise Man, he would finally be able to accommodate himself to the world:

> The Wise Man, when abroad,
> Impartial to the world,
> Does not divide or judge.
> But people everywhere
> Mark well his ears and eyes;
> For wise men hear and see
> As little children do.
>
> (*Tao Tê Ching,* p. 102)

But ultimately humor, like Zen and Tao, defies analysis.[7] The Treatise

[7]Seng Ts'an can only suggest Zen:

> Space is bright, but self-illumined; no power of mind is exerted.
> Nor indeed could mere thought bring us to such a place.
> Nor could sense or feeling comprehend it.
> It is the Truly-so, the Transcendent Sphere, where there is neither He nor I.
>
> (*Teachings of the Compassionate Buddha,* p. 230)

Lao Tzu's description of Tao is even less explicit:

> They call it elusive, and say,
> That one looks
> But it never appears.
> They say that indeed it is rare,
> Since one listens
> But never a sound.
> Subtle, they call it, and say
> That one grasps it
> But never gets hold.
> These three complaints amount
> To only one, which is
> Beyond all resolution.
>
> (*Tao Tê Ching,* p. 66)

informs Harry that he must live in the world as if he were an Immortal, but it is for Harry to determine how he will accomplish this feat, like the Zen novitiate who spends years meditating on paradoxical *koans* to obtain a single experience of satori. The Treatise is aware of the difficult charge it is placing on Harry; but it also insists that Harry is an exceptional man who, while he cannot transcend as the saint/sinner, is still worthy of the high ideal of humor. It is just because the Steppenwolf is so advanced that he suffers as he does. The Treatise advises Harry to live with his brother bourgeois, but only as a means of crossing over to the Immortals:

> No, we are speaking of man in the highest sense, of the end of the long road to true manhood, of kingly men, of the Immortals. . . . Harry has, we should say, genius enough to attempt the quest of true manhood instead of discoursing pitifully about his stupid Steppenwolf at every difficulty encountered.

Harry, then, is offered release from underground, but only if he remakes himself. The tired and sardonic Steppenwolf, however, resolves that rather than undergo another painful "reorganization, another incarnation," he will simply put an end to his life. But whatever the origin of the Treatise—whether it be a "magical" revelation made to Harry by the Immortals or merely a fleeting intuition which he himself has—he suspects it may be accurate; and like Plato's cave dweller who gets his first glimpse of the sun, once Harry has seen his own flickering light he will never again be able to ignore it. As yet, however, the Treatise addresses itself only to his intellect. It must now insinuate itself into his heart and will. This is accomplished, or almost accomplished, with the help of the two other principal characters in the novel, Hermine and Pablo, and the marvelous events of the Magic Theatre.

One of the most dramatic moments of the novel is the first meeting between Harry and Hermine. After a harrowing day that drives Harry to the brink of suicide, he enters a cabaret. Disheveled, bespotted with mud, an anxious and desperate expression on his face, he works his way to the bar, at which sits a "pale and pretty girl." Almost instinctively he sits beside her and immediately begins to unburden himself to her, like a distressed child who runs to the arms of its mother. She, in turn, proceeds to reveal all sorts of things about him which he recognizes as true, and Harry feels that he has known her all his life. When he asks her her name, she tells him to guess it; he recognizes it as Hermine because she reminds him of a boyhood friend whose name is Herman. (The name-play is obvious: Hermine,

Herman, Hermann Hesse, Harry Haller.) She tells Harry, "I am a kind of looking glass for you because there is something in me that answers you and understands you."

Hermine appears to be uncanny because, even though she is an actual flesh-and-blood "character" in the novel, she functions as the personification of Harry's feminine nature. (At one point she suggests to him that she might be a boy in woman's clothing.) Hesse, of course, was familiar with the inseparability of the feminine *yin* from the masculine *yang* in Taoist philosophy. But the unique crystallization of Harry's feminine side in the form of Hermine suggests C. G. Jung's *anima*. Jung's influence on Hesse can hardly be doubted.[8] The substance of the Treatise is at the core of Jung's thinking. But it is chiefly his analytic method, roughly as it was practiced in his clinic in Zurich, that Hesse took over in *Steppenwolf*. Jung offers the means of realizing in practice the lofty mandates of the Treatise. Therefore, before we focus on Hermine as anima, we ought briefly to consider Jung's psychology as a whole.

In common with Zen and Taoism, the basic concept in Jung's system is balance, often expressed by the figure of the *mandala*. Jung conceives of the psyche as a composite of dynamic polarities. Man possesses, for example, four contrary functions—intellect, emotion, sensation and intuition—any one of which is apt to be neglected when another is overdeveloped. Harmony is also demanded between the objective world outside and the *unconscious* within, with both of which he (more precisely, his *ego,* or *consciousness*) continually interacts. To adjust to the outside world—with its laws, conventions and social pressures—man develops an appropriate mask, or *persona.* Counterparts to the persona are the anima (a man's feminine nature) and the *animus* (a woman's masculine nature), which function like filters between the ego and the unconscious; the persona and the anima (or animus) constitute still another polarized relationship. Even within the unconscious there is an interchange between what Jung calls the *personal unconscious* and the *collective unconscious*—the first containing all the buried memories and attitudes that an individual, and only that individual, has acquired in his lifetime; the latter, like the Indian world-soul, encompassing images and thought patterns common to all men at all times (i.e., *archetypes*). Finally, there is a dynamic tension between the ego and the *Self.*

---

[8] Hesse's personal friendship with Jung, the Jungian therapy that Hesse underwent and his characterization of it as the "hellish journey through myself," the recurrence of the anima figure in his writings after that therapy, and, finally, his frank acknowledgments of his debt to Jung—all are documented facts which we need not belabor here.

The ego, which is mere consciousness, is limited in its comprehension of internal reality; the Self, which embraces all of the above psychic elements, is an apprehension – transcending yet including consciousness – of the entire psyche grasped as a unity.

Ideally, the Self is the center of a balanced constellation that embraces all of the other psychic functions and "parts," and the aim of Jungian therapy is to achieve maximum realization of Self through the harmonious ordering of its parts. The ego-consciousness can never grasp the Self in its entirety. But through the growing awareness of the outside world (experience), and through cumulative insight into the unconscious (therapy), it learns to differentiate between attitudes that "fit" into the whole system and those that tend to disrupt it, thus acquiring what the Treatise would call humor. The process by which this is achieved Jung has termed *individuation,* by which man becomes a "psychological 'individual,' that is, a separate unity or 'whole.' "[9]

To achieve individuation; to integrate the Treatise's "bundle of selves" (Jung's *shadow selves*); to develop an effective mask (Jung's persona) in order to live in bourgeois society; and, finally, to achieve satori (for Jung, the sudden upsurge of the unconscious into the conscious) without losing his sanity, Harry must first turn inward – not so much like the immobile Indian yogi in meditation as like the hectic Western man in psychotherapy. He must, in other words, come to terms with the anima.

According to Jung, the anima is the bridge between consciousness and unconsciousness, determining what signals pass from the one to the other. Only through direct confrontation with the "woman" in him can a man come to know what is welling in the depths of his mind, particularly how he feels about things as distinguished from the way he conceptualizes them:

> Woman, with her very dissimilar psychology, is and always has been
> a source of information about things for which a man has no eyes. She
> can be his inspiration; her intuitive capacity, often superior to a
> man's, can give him timely warning, and her feeling, always directed

---

[9] C. G. Jung, *Collected Works: The Archetypes and the Collective Unconscious,* London, 1959, Vol. 9, Pt. 1, p. 275. Jung's use of the term individuation should not be confused with Hesse's.

towards the personal, can show him ways which his own less personally accented feeling would never have discovered.[10]

If all men need the supplemental vision of the anima, the radically isolated Steppenwolf is in particular need of it. Although the Treatise expresses the dictates of Harry's basic being, his understanding of them is, as we have seen, merely intellectual and therefore superficial. Only on meeting Hermine, i.e., facing the anima objectified as an autonomous personality, does he begin to accept the teachings of the Treatise with emotional conviction. As he attempted to brush aside the Treatise, so Harry now "resists" Hermine's promptings. But she is not so easily denied, for she speaks not from the top of his head, as it were, but from the profoundest recesses of his soul. Harry's alternative, then, is to face her and come to some understanding with her or, as in his case thus far, suffer from the inexplicable moods and "affects" of which she is the personification. To achieve self-realization, and thus free himself from these moods, Harry must, in the words of Jung,

... become conscious of his invisible system of relations to the unconscious, and especially of the anima, so as to be able to distinguish himself from her. (*Two Essays,* p. 198-199)

*   *   *

Immediately after meeting Hermine, Harry begins to look within. Her first command is that he take a nap. He falls asleep and dreams that he is visiting Goethe (that day he had an argument with someone as to the true nature of the great poet, whom he considers one of the Immortals). In the dream Harry proceeds to reprimand Goethe for having compromised with the bourgeoisie. Goethe laughs his crystal laugh at Harry, telling him that he takes himself too seriously and that he too must learn to laugh. Goethe also executes a neat dance step, despite his age (Hermine has just chastized Harry for not knowing how to dance). Then the wily old poet reveals a tiny box that contains a diminutive reproduction of a woman's leg. Harry's buried sexual urge is aroused (he has already begun to desire Hermine). Impulsively, he reaches out to take the leg; but the leg squirms—it is a scorpion—and Harry recoils in terror. The dream functions like the Treatise by revealing to Harry his deficiencies: he lacks a sense of humor, he has

[10] C. G. Jung, *Two Essays in Analytical Psychology,* New York, 1956, p. 198-199.

ignored his body, he has an ambivalent attitude toward sex. But the dream, unlike the Treatise, is a direct revelation of the unconscious.

In the next few weeks Hermine takes Harry in hand. She points out to him that though he has developed his intellect to an uncommon extent, he is inept in the elementary business of living; that he is shy and awkward with people; that he is incapable of enjoying the simple pleasures of the senses; that he has shamefully abused his body:

> In your case, for example, the spiritual part is very highly developed, and so you are very backward in all the little arts of living. Harry, the thinker, is a hundred years old, but Harry, the dancer, is scarcely half a day old. It's he we want to bring on, and all his little brothers who are just as little and stupid as he is.

Her first command is that he learn to dance. Accordingly he buys a gramaphone—which he has always detested—and daily practices the fox trot under Hermine's guidance. Slowly, painfully, his clumsy and reluctant body begins to respond. Soon he is able to appear on a public dance floor. Self-conscious, embarrassed, always ready to quit and return to his hermitage, he is checked by the mocking laughter of Hermine (Jung would call her "She-who-must-be-obeyed"). (*Two Essays,* p. 199) Soon he is a familiar figure in the cabarets and ballrooms, those twin abominations of modern society that the old Steppenwolf so often reviled. He also becomes more conscious of dress, of the pleasures of eating, of the innumerable little wordly things that he previously underestimated.

To complete his metamorphosis into a worldling, Harry must learn the art of love. Hermine has decreed that sexual intimacy between Harry and herself must be deferred until he is unconditionally in love with her. Meanwhile, in her role as anima, she must procure for him what he needs now: simple, uncomplicated sex. Moreover, she must select the woman for him, since it is always the anima that determines what woman a man gravitates toward. So she selects for him a skillful and sympathetic prostitute (a Western parallel to the courtesan Kamala in *Siddhartha*), her friend Maria.

Maria is a simple, beautiful animal. Uneducated, uninhibited, her whole life is oriented around the sensual:

> All her art and the whole task she set herself lay in extracting the utmost delight from the senses she had been endowed with, and from

her particular figure, her color, her hair, her voice, her skin, her temperament; and in employing every faculty, every curve and line and every softest modeling of her body to find responsive perceptions in her lovers and to conjure up in them an answering quickness of delight.

Harry proves to be an apt and responsive pupil, as he abandons himself to the delights of pure sensuality. Whole new worlds, radiant and transfigured, open up to him in Maria's arms. Yet they are not entirely unfamiliar: the ecstasy he experiences corresponds to the emotions evoked in him by that "divine track" which he has always associated exclusively with the Immortals. In fact, he learns that body and spirit are not irreconcilable antitheses but friendly complements within a single system. Thus as his body quickens into life, images of forgotten women spring into consciousness. Memories of his mother, of the wife who had deserted him, of the "women whom I had loved, desired and sung, whose love I had seldom won and seldom striven to win," are revived. He discovers that Eros is no stranger to him, but that he had merely buried the potential lover in him for many loveless years because the women in his life had caused him pain. But now, through Maria, he is able to accept them as precious parts of himself:

Indestructible and abiding as the stars, these experiences, though forgotten, could never be erased. Their series was the story of my life, their starry light the undying value of my being.

His reconciliation with the women of his past marks his union with the total Woman, or anima. Hermine, the anima, incorporates Maria, the purely physical female. So Maria relinquishes Harry at the time appointed for his "possession" of Hermine, the night of the Masked Ball.

This night is crucial. Having failed to find Hermine at the ball, Harry lapses into his old despair and prepares to leave. Suddenly he sees another mysterious notice of the Magic Theatre, only this one includes mention of Hermine:

Tonight at the Magic Theatre
For Madmen Only
Price of Admittance Your Mind
Not for Everybody
Hermine in Hell

Hell, as it turns out, is a downstairs room at the ball decorated as the Inferno. But symbolically it is Harry's unconscious mind, over which Hermine has thus far had possession. To reach her, then, he must descend into his unconscious, where the "hell" is. But now he is both able and willing to make the descent: he is ready for Hermine. When he does go to her he finds, not a severe and mocking mentor, but an acquiescent woman whom he takes in his arms and kisses for the first time: "I was hers, and her way of dancing, her looks and smiles and kisses all showed that she gave herself to me." As they dance their "nuptial" dance, Harry realizes that all of the women he had ever known "had melted together and become one, the one whom I held in my arms." Never has he been as happy as he is now, in anticipation of Hermine's surrender.

But Harry is not destined to possess Hermine. He is sidetracked by Pablo and the Magic Theatre.

Like Hermine, Pablo functions as both an objective character and as a personification of psychic elements in Harry. However, Harry is slow to realize his kinship with Pablo. Throughout most of the novel, he views Pablo as his opposite. He sees him as essentially a male counterpart of Maria, in other words, as a faun-like creature that pleases women in bed:

> No, he said nothing, this Señor Pablo, nor did he even appear to think much, this charming caballero. His business was with the saxophone in the jazz-band and to this calling he appeared to devote himself with love and passion. Often during the course of the music he would suddenly clap with his hands, or permit himself other expressions of enthusiasm, such as, singing out "O O O, Ha Ha, Hallo." Apart from this, however, he confined himself to being beautiful, to pleasing women, to wearing collars and ties of the latest fashion and a great number of rings on his fingers.

But Harry's smug sense of superiority is slowly undermined as he begins to discover other qualities in Pablo. Pablo seems to be simple; yet he is in perfect harmony with his environment and at absolute peace with himself. He does not appear to have studied psychology; yet instantly upon meeting Harry he knows that Harry is unhappy and lacks a sense of humor! Pablo has not written books exposing social injustice; yet he is continually alleviating the very real suffering around him. Paradoxically and (given Hesse's mischievous sense of humor) deliberately, the author has created in this seemingly insignificant saxophonist—as he does in the "servant" Leo in *Journey to the East*—the enlightened disciple of Zen and Taoism.

Pablo has arrived where Harry should be—where, in fact, he actually begins aspiring to be after meeting Hermine:

> ... what I needed was not knowledge and understanding. What I longed for in my despair was life and resolution, action and reaction, impulse and impetus.

These are essentially masculine characteristics. But Pablo also possesses feminine qualities—sensitivity, delicacy, a quick intuition. As a matter of fact, just as the masculine element is stressed in Hermine, so the feminine is conspicuous in Pablo who, like her, is bisexual and actually suggests on one occasion that Harry, Maria and himself engage in a love-game for three. Pablo, in a word, is the perfect man because his male and female counterparts, the *yin* and the *yang,* are in perfect balance. Lao Tzu need not warn him:

> Be aware of your masculine nature;
> But by keeping the feminine way,
> You shall be to the world like a canyon,
> Where the Virtue eternal abides,
> And go back to become as a child.
>
> (*Tao Tê Ching,* p. 80)

Understandably, then, Pablo replaces Hermine as Harry's guide through the Magic Theatre (which, significantly, transpires in an upstairs room, thus implying Harry's "ascent"). There Pablo will appear not only in his "real" form, but also as an Eastern guru.

Like the Buddhist Hui-neng (who saw in his own mind a reflection of the universe and was therefore called the Zen Master of the Great Mirror), Harry is ready to plunge into the rich "picture gallery" in his own soul, even more deeply than he did under Hermine's tutelage. However, to enter the theatre he must surrender himself to magic and fantasy, the price of admission being his excessively rational, excessively intellectual mind. Accordingly, he takes a drug and commits symbolic suicide: he looks into a mirror, which reflects his conscious conception of himself—his own image encircled by a wolf—and with a laugh he shatters it. He is thus emulating the Zen adept who attempts to penetrate beneath reason and to intuit reality wholly and spontaneously; at the same time, he is embarking on a psychedelic trip, which has essentially the same purpose.[11] Pablo, who provides him the drug, will act both as the veteran drug user accompanying the initiate on his first trip as well as the Zen master in *sanzen*, the conference between disciple and master on the former's progress

The Magic Theatre itself is an elaborate fantasy resembling an extended dream. It consists of a sequence of apparently absurd events, or "entertainments," following one after the other, linked by association rather than by logic, centering around either Harry himself (the dreamer) or some aspect of him represented by other figures (shadow selves and archetypes). The significance of the events enacted in the Magic Theatre lies less in their meaning than in their manner of presentation. Their meaning has already been anticipated by the Treatise and by Hermine; but now it is being reiterated with a force generated from the deepest layers of Harry's mind. They are a recapitulation of several relationships, all of them involving some kind of imbalance: Harry's relationship to society, to women, to the other "Harry's" within him, and to the Immortals.

Harry's conflict with society is treated in several entertainments. In "Jolly Hunting," he sees himself involved in a revolution directed against the bourgeois plutocrat and his technology, which, in real life, Haller has criticized in his books and articles. The purpose of this "just" war is to destroy all machines, which threaten soon to make the modern world uninhabitable (the time is in the Twenties!). However, as he begins to kill people indiscriminately, he realizes that his reformer's zeal is only a guise under which is concealed a blind and murderous impulse, and he feels a kinship with the generals from whom he had so disdainfully dissociated himself: "Pah—all that blood! We were ashamed of ourselves. But in the war there must have been generals even who felt the same." The implication of this adventure is reinforced in another entertainment, the "Marvelous Taming of the Steppenwolf." To compensate for the savagery of the wolf and the overrefinement of the man in him, Harry witnesses in this scene (which is of course created by him) a wolf acting like a human and a man like a beast. But the bestial man and the human wolf are so exaggerated, and their unnatural roles presented with such obvious cruelty, that Harry can only wonder once more at his presumption in damning the bellicosity of the German bourgeoisie:

---

[11] Timothy Leary claims that drugs offer a shortcut to satori by activating vast complexes of brain cells in us that are ordinarily inactive.

Today I knew that no tamer of beasts, no general, no insane person
could hatch a thought or a picture in his brain that I could not match
myself with one every bit as frightful, every bit as savage and wicked,
as crude and stupid.

Not only does Harry realize that he is in no moral position to judge, but
he also comes to see that he is a part of the society of his day and must
therefore share its guilt. Thus he has a vision of Brahms and Wagner—who
in their day held opposing views about music—now working out penance
for the same fault, thick orchestration. He learns that this is a fault of the
times, for which these composers must assume responsibility. Indeed,
Harry learns that he is responsible not just for the sins of contemporary
society but for "Adam and the apple, and the whole of original sin": he
carries within him both the immediate environment (Jung's *collectivity*)
and the history of the race (collective unconscious). Along with the
believers in certain Hindu and Buddhist sects, he is jolted into the
awareness that no matter how enlightened he becomes, he must postpone
his own nirvana, his own reunion with the Immortals, until the racial
karma has been worked out. To be a complete person he must acknowledge
his integral attachment to the whole human race instead of vacillating
between the superhuman Immortals and the subhuman wolf. Even if he
wants to, Harry cannot really be an outcast.

Harry's relation to "himself" is the subject of the performance
"Guidance in the Building of the Personality. Success Guaranteed." The
pieces of a smashed mirror, which earlier reflected many different
images of him, now become his potential selves (Jung's shadow selves):
". . . old men and young men and children and women, cheerful and sad,
strong and weak, nimble and clumsy," in each of which he recognizes his
essential Self. Under the guidance of a wizard (in the person of Pablo), he
learns how to rearrange them into various life configurations such as
"groups and families, games and battles, friendships and enmities, making
a small world." The guru tells him:

This is the art of life. You may yourself as an artist develop the game
of your life and lend it animation. You may complicate and enrich it
as you please. It lies in your hands.

Like the river in *Siddhartha,* the League archives in *Journey to the East,* and the bead game in *The Glass Bead Game,* the game here functions as a symbol of the one in the many, of unity in variety; it combines, in addition, Jung's collective unconscious and the Hindu doctrine of karma and reincarnation. Hesse once remarked, "The act of dying is like falling into Jung's collective unconscious and from there you return to form, to pure form."[12] To "die" is simply to discard one form and assume another one from the vast reservoir of forms, i.e., archetypal images, that the individual carries around within him, the selection of his new self being determined by his psychic development at the time of his death. The Treatise has already urged Harry to "kill" the restrictive Steppenwolf and re-create himself; but whereas he had first resolved that he would not make another painful metamorphosis, he is now eager to play this chess game of life for "whole eternities."

Harry's sexual life is explored in another entertainment, "All Girls Are Yours." This fantasy is essentially a dramatic reenactment of the memories Maria had awakened in him. But instead of merely reflecting on the women of his past, he now interacts with them, and this time successfully. Thus what was so painful to him that he had to repress it, is now idyllic. Maria and Hermine have made him realize the ways in which he had bungled with women; the wizard he has just left—the chess pieces are still warm in his pocket—has taught him that he need not repeat his past mistakes and that he can assume any role he chooses. Consequently, as he lives in imagination his past romances, from budding adolescence to the present, he is the perfect lover: "All the love that I had missed in my life bloomed magically in my garden during this hour of dreams."

Harry feels the elation and self-confidence of the lover again, just as he did at the end of the ball. And once again, he is ready to consummate the chief love of his life by taking Hermine. But once again, Pablo intrudes. To his dismay, Harry discovers Pablo and Hermine lying naked in one another's arms after having made love. Without a moment's hesitation, Harry runs a knife through Hermine's heart.

We can only conjecture as to why Harry kills his beloved, since Hesse does not explicitly give a reason. We might explain Harry's folly as simple jealousy, coupled with a regression to his old bourgeois sense of honor. We might interpret it as a fulfillment of the unspoken promise he made earlier to Hermine that he would obey her last command, which was to kill her,

---

[12] Miguel Serrano, *C. G. Jung and Hermann Hesse: A Record of Two Friendships,* tr. Frank MacShane, New York, 1966, p. 4.

and that she was simply expressing that command by deliberately allowing herself to be caught in Pablo's arms. But surely this incident has a symbolical meaning as well, since everything that happens in the theatre reveals something about Harry's psyche. Again, we must turn to Jung.

The patient in Jungian therapy strives to free himself from subjection to the unconscious as expressed by the anima. Until he confronts her, she exerts a mysterious power, or *mana,* over him. As Harry (the ego) enters into an honest dialogue with Hermine (the anima), she begins to relinquish this mana and he in turn begins to exert an influence over her. Hermine knows that while she can teach Harry much about his emotions and the "little arts of living" (which are the domain of the anima), she can learn from Harry about the world of ideas and spirit, the *logos* with which the animus is more at ease). Thus in the beginning of their relationship she is Harry's tutor and he does little more than follow her bidding; as their friendship progresses, however, she adopts more and more of Harry's original attitudes, for example, his impatience with this world and his longing for death and the Immortals. Harry observes of their last serious conversation together:

> It seemed to me that it was not, perhaps, her own thoughts but mine. She had read them like a clairvoyant, breathed them in and given them back, so that they had a form of their own and came to me as something new.

We may even assume that Hermine's unspoken command that Harry kill her was also his psychic suggestion; for as we have seen, in his ambivalence about life, he wants to obey the life-restoring Hermine but at the same time perversely resists her and wishes to be rid of her.

At the point when Harry and Hermine have a mutual effect on each other, their relationship is in perfect balance. But as he grows in self-confidence, he attempts to appropriate the mana from Hermine, that is, dominate the anima. He becomes what is for Jung the *mana-personality,* thereby exposing himself to subjugation from another source, what Jung calls the archetype of the superman:

> But the mana-personality is a dominant of the collective unconscious, the recognized archetype of the mighty man in the form of hero, chief, magician, medicine man, saint, the ruler of man and spirits, the friend of God. . . . Hence the "magician" could only take possession of the ego because the ego dreamed of victory over the anima. (*Two Essays,* p. 240)

Harry, we will recall, was just about ready to possess Hermine at the end of the Masked Ball. At last, he felt himself to be the master. In the Magic Theatre he experiences this sense of power again, first in the "chess game" with the guru and, next, during his infallible performance with the women in "All Girls Are Yours." When he sees Hermine in the arms of Pablo, he symbolically asserts his mastery over Hermine by stabbing her. But he fails to realize that the naked Pablo is really his own masculine self, which Hermine has helped him to fashion, and that Hermine is his feminine self. The beautiful picture formed by Pablo and Hermine—which Harry himself describes in some of the most lyrical prose of the novel—is an image of the ideal Harry, whose feminine and masculine counterparts have merged into perfect union. Or, stating the premise in reverse, we can say that this picture cancels out sexual differentiation—another of Harry's dichotomies—and depicts the sexless condition of the Immortals. Hermine, like Underground Man's Liza, offers salvation: to kill her would be absurd. Fortunately, as Harry learns later, the Hermine he has stabbed is only an illusion, like everything else in the Magic Theatre.

Harry should have known, even before the night of the Magic Theatre, that a man cannot abuse the anima without seriously harming himself. In fact, he cannot ever master the anima. He cannot keep Hermine from going to Pablo; nor is he in control of his emotions, i.e., the anima, when he impulsively "kills" Hermine only to regret the act afterwards. It should not be a question of mastery between the ego and the anima, says Jung, for any attempt on the part of one to dominate the other results in imbalance:

> . . . the anima has forfeited her tyranical power to the extent the ego was able to come to terms with the unconscious. This accommodation, however, was not a victory of the conscious over the unconscious, but the establishment of a balance of power between two worlds. (*Two Essays,* pp. 241-242)

But the question still remains: What, properly, is the fate of the mana, that vital force without which we are nothing? According to Jung, it ideally falls to the Self,

> . . . something that is both conscious and unconscious, or else neither. This something is the desired "mid-point" of the personality, that ineffable something betwixt the opposites, or else that which unites them, or the result of conflict, or the product of energetic tension: the

coming to birth of personality, a profoundly individual step forward, the next stage. (*Two Essays,* p. 242)

Thus Self-realization is the reconciliation of opposites within the psyche. Only when Harry has achieved this condition will he acquire that calm, philosophic attitude that the Treatise describes as a sense of humor. At the end of the novel, he still has a long way to go; however, he has made considerable progress since his first reading of the Treatise—he has gone well beyond underground man. The society of his day is still alarmingly headed for disaster, but despite the social folly, Harry has come to realize his own faults as more urgent. Beginning with the Treatise, he has begun to look inward; Hermine has introduced him to his unconscious and Pablo has led him through its darker labyrinths. He has come to appreciate his complexity and contradictions, and he is determined at least to live with them, if not actually resolve them. His final vow, though humble and inconclusive, represents an affirmation of life that the old suicidal Steppenwolf would have been incapable of making:

> I knew that all the hundred thousand pieces of life's game were in my pocket. A glimpse of its meaning had stirred my reason and I was determined to begin the game afresh. I would sample its tortures once more and shudder again at its senselessness. I would traverse not once more, but often, the hell of my inner being.

Underground man, an unbeliever who would like to believe, would find slight satisfaction in Hesse's unabashed mysticism. Even in his deepest despair Harry has faith in the Absolute (the Immortals), and he probably would be unwilling to make the effort called for by the Treatise if he did not hope to achieve through it the blissful condition of the Immortals. In other words, in order to develop the sense of humor which makes life endurable, Harry must first have faith in an overall pattern and unity in the universe. The problem with underground man, on the other hand, is to learn how to survive without that a priori justification which faith provides. As Dostoevsky's Underground Man knew, if one does not have faith to begin with, how does he deliberately go about acquiring it without exposing himself to what Sartre will later describe as "bad faith"? Finally, even if we could will ourselves into a state of belief, humor is, as the Treatise explicitly points out, obtainable only to men of genius and demands a "martyrdom of spirit" which few geniuses, short of Kierkegaard's Knight of Faith, will submit to. Hence aside from Siddhartha–who is literally the Buddha– none of Hesse's blood-and-bone heroes ever achieves the satori that resides in humor; only minor characters–the ethereal Magister Musicae in *The Glass Bead Game* or idealized Leo in *Journey to the East*–approach it in their lifetime.

That other "believer," the revolutionary, would be even less inspired by the conclusion of *Steppenwolf.* He would interpret Hesse's sense of humor as passive resignation that encourages one to offer the other cheek when there are only too many people ready to slap it. The revolutionist is totally committed to a single end. Prepared to lay down his life for it, he would doubtlessly equate himself with Hesse's saint (which his enemies would call sinner), rather than with Hesse's mandarin of humor. But does humor, as Hesse defines it, necessarily preclude action? On the one hand, the ideal of the Japanese *samurai* and karate masters, who were presumably trained in the Zen equivalent of humor, is action–to strike at the right moment, and always with deadly precision. On the other hand, it is difficult to imagine a radical revolutionary who is not fundamentally motivated by anger, which by definition contradicts Hesse's humor. Hesse himself distinguishes humor from the extremes of saintliness and sinning. For humor, after all, encourages accommodation to the bourgeois status quo, whereas revolution is directed at its destruction. Since Hesse is deliberately unexplicit in his treatment of humor, we can only speculate whether one can kill with a smile![13]

But in the final analysis, most readers are neither avowed skeptics, on the one hand, nor passionate believers in God or other absolutes on the other. They want simply to live. Therefore, they are concerned more with a style of living than with a raison d'être. It is to them that the bourgeois Steppenwolf (in search of an unbourgeois soul) makes his perennial appeal. Hesse ultimately speaks to those Steppenwolfian critics of life who are nonetheless unwilling to part with it. For them the Immortals need not be literal creatures inhabiting an actual realm from which mortals are categorically excluded but, rather, an ideal state of mind which, as in Harry's case, the diligent seeker might never attain but can continually draw nearer to. Such readers see in the Treatise a tempering of the ego (so precious to Western man) and a call for awareness and adaptability and, in exchange, the promise of a fuller life. With Harry, who obliterates the

---

[13]This question will be dealt with at greater length in Chapter 7.

image of Steppenwolf in the mirror, they know they will not go underground as long as they open themselves to the infinite possibilities both within themselves and the world without. With Harry, they can make the vow, Oriental in its essence, of that patient of Jung who wrote:

> I always thought that, when we accept things, they overpower us in one way or another. Now this is not true at all, and it is only by accepting them that one can define an attitude toward them. So now I intend playing the *game of life* [italics added], being receptive to whatever comes to me, good and bad, sun and shadow that are forever shifting, and, in this way, also accepting my own nature with its positive and negative sides. Thus everything becomes more alive to me. What a fool I was! How I tried to force everything to go according to my idea![14]

---

[14] C. G. Jung and Richard Wilhelm, *The Secret of the Golden Flower,* London, 1931, p. 126.

UNDERGROUND MAN AND THE VOID

Chapter 4

Jean-Paul Sartre: *Being and Nothingness* and *Nausea*

Dostoevsky, Kafka and Hesse portray underground man as a hapless individual who dislikes himself for good reasons and the society of his day for probably better ones. But each of these writers reduces the psychological and social causes of underground man's discontent to the more basic fact of his divorce from God. The alternatives they offer are, simply, religious fulfillment or underground. Sartre, like Camus and Genet, considers God (if He does exist) to be irrelevant. Today, along with the remaining writers we shall take up, he puts considerably more emphasis on the social genesis of underground man than did Dostoevsky, Kafka and Hesse. Twenty-five years ago, however, Sartre stressed man's condition. But whether underground man is seen as part of a group or in isolation, his dilemma according to Sartre is purely human; and if any resolution is possible, it must be in this world.

Today, Sartre is a declared Marxist.[1] Thus he joins those legions of intellectuals who, as we shall see later, turned to revolution instead of God as a means of coping with underground. But despite his widely publicized activities as a Marxist—his agitation for the liberation of Algiers, his championing of student dissent on the Sorbonne campus, his rejection of the "reactionary" Nobel Prize, his leadership (along with Bertrand Russell) of the War Crimes Tribunal which tried Lyndon B. Johnson in effigy—Sartre's name will always be associated with Existentialism. Sartre's unique

---

[1] He ascribes his initial ignorance of Marx (and Freud) to the faulty education to which he and the other "petty-bourgeois" intellectuals of his day were exposed. ("An Interview with Sartre," first published in *New Left Review*, No. 58, reprinted in *The New York Review of Books*, XIV, Number 6, March 26, 1970, pp. 22-31.)

formulation of Existentialism, suggested first in the novel *Nausea* (1938) and then systematically developed in the philosophic tome *Being and Nothingness* (1943), has assumed a permanent place in the academy and become a battle cry for millions of youths since World War II. Indeed, despite those critics who hold that Marxism and Existentialism are contradictory, Sartre's political involvement today was already foreshadowed in *Being and Nothingness,* which argues that man's only salvation in a universe abandoned by God is, not consistency, but personal commitment.[2] Many novelists besides Malraux have shown underground man turning to Marx for salvation. But only Sartre has depicted underground man as an Existentialist, first in the neophytic form of Roquentin in *Nausea* and then as the finely etched and complete product of the philosophical work *Being and Nothingness.*

BEING AND NOTHINGNESS

Sartre makes a fundamental distinction between *being-in-itself* (Being) and *being-for-itself.* Being-in-itself is what it is; it is not in the process of becoming something else. It is uncreated and uncaused (God could not have created Being since God himself is Being); nor is it directed at some future possibility inasmuch as it can never become anything other than what it is. In other words, being-in-itself is absolute—without origin, causality or direction. We perceive Being in the form of individual objects and events. These particular beings (*existants*) come and go, exhibit spatial and temporal dimension, follow laws of cause and effect, lend themselves to measurement and categorization. For example, the seed bears fruit; the fruit in time rots on the bough and disintegrates. But the seed and the fruit, as well as the physical chemical laws that govern them, are only manifestations of the single Being. They are to being-in-itself what the foam on the surface of the ocean is to the ocean.

Insofar as man is a biological organism he is part of being-in-itself. But what is uniquely human in man is his consciousness, through which he can detach himself from Being. Consciousness is not a fixed repository for ideas and perceptions (such as memory); rather, it is a process, an activity, a perpetual reaching out to its object without ever merging with it.

---

[2] The criticism of Sartre's quixotic alliance with the Communists is briefly examined in Nicola Chiarmonte's "Sartre Versus Camus: a Political Quarrel" (from *Camus,* ed. Germaine Brée, in the series *Twentieth Century Views,* New York, 1962, pp. 31-37). The focus of the article is on the break between Sartre and Camus over the issue of Communism.

Consciousness is aware of itself as separated and distinct from its object, which, relative to consciousness, is always an in-itself. Consciousness is, instead, a being-*for*-itself, i.e., a *non*-Being (in-itself). Therefore man, *as consciousness,* is that "being such that in its being [consciousness], its being is in question in so far as this being implies a being other than itself [being-in-itself]."[3]

This negative function of consciousness is best illustrated in man's unique capacity to ask questions. Every question presupposes the possibility of a negative response. If I ask, for example, "Is John at home now?," I allow for the possibility of his *not being* at home. I have conceived of *not-being,* as if I had punctured a hole in the self-contained fullness of being-in-itself. Of course being-in-itself is actually independent of any question I ask—it is what it is whether John is at home or not at home. Nonetheless, to the questioner Nothingness is real: it is a subjective, *human reality,* being-for-itself as distinguished from being-in-itself. Every question, every notion of negation, destruction, absence, lack, incompletion, and so on, presupposes both the fullness of Being and the reality of Nothingness. Through questioning, Sartre holds, man "secretes nothingness" between himself and Being:

> Thus, in so far as the questioner must be able to effect in relation to the questioned a *nihilating withdrawal,* he is not subject to the causal order of the world: he detaches himself from Being.

Man, then, is "that Being which is its own Nothingness."

Being-in-itself is prior to and independent of consciousness—it is not something we imagine. It is also unlimited and undifferentiated. However, our experience of Being, as distinguished from Being itself, is conditioned by our consciousness. Consciousness is like a sieve through which Being flows. As Being passes through consciousness, i.e., as we perceive it, it takes on form, becomes separate objects with specific dimensions and relations, admits of limits, observes mechanical laws, and so on. Although *in fact* it is what it is in spite of us, *for* us being-in-itself becomes a recognizable, viz., human world. It becomes, in short, what we "choose" it to be. Actually, of course, it need not conform to our interpretation of it; thus approaching a lion as if he were a pussycat would be a mistake. But the phenomenon "lion," a label designating the synthesis of the lion's mass, color, sound, movement, and so forth, is an abstraction from the totality of Being. That abstraction, whether we label it "lion" or "cat," "harmful" or "harmless," is an operation of human consciousness.[4]

All that man can be certain of is that he exists and that he exists in the world (the *situation*). Since God is dead (or, at best, has *abandoned* man), man must define the meaning of both himself and the world. Meaning and value, then, are strictly human. Moreover, since whatever impinges on us from without must pass through the filter of individual consciousness, each of us experiences the world subjectively. Whatever Being may be in itself, we apprehend it as ours, and ours alone. The world becomes, for each of us, a miniature constellation with ourselves as centers. This is what Sartre means when he says that each of us is responsible not just for himself but for the whole world as well.

When through "nihilating withdrawal" man separates himself from the "causal order" of Being, he takes on an awesome freedom. As a matter of fact, this withdrawal *is* his freedom; man, in his lack of being-in-itself, is by definition free:

> What we call freedom is impossible to distinguish from the *being* of "human reality." Man does not exist *first* in order to be free subsequently; there is no difference between the being of man and his *being-free*.

Unlike an object, which is what it is, man only "is" (more precisely, is becoming) what he makes himself through active choice. ("Existence precedes essence.") Sartre contends that human action, unlike natural phenomena, are never "caused": we cannot refer our actions to God, Freudian complexes, heredity, environment, or anything else not rooted in freedom and consciousness. He denies, in *Being and Nothingness,* that a man is a criminal because he grew up in a certain environment or that he is miserable because he was born with a serious hereditary disease. Neither the childhood environment nor the physical handicap are "given" to a man as the hump is to the camel: a camel would not be a camel without a hump. A man's heredity and environment, on the other hand, are subject to his adaptation and transformation. He puts his personal stamp on them, defines them and adopts a specific attitude toward them. In *choosing* himself he chooses them—he could always unequivocally reject them by committing suicide, for example. Thus though heredity and environment exist as

---

[4] Sartre does not concern himself with the consciousness of animals.

brute facts, their meaning is always human; and since action always involves choice (human reality is frighteningly moral for Sartre), a man must bear the full responsibility for them.[5]

The realization of this responsibility, for Sartre, is *anguish*: "In anguish I apprehend myself as totally free and not being able to derive the meaning of the world except as coming from myself." Since freedom is Nothingness (it is *not* being-in-itself), then the freedom to do something admits at the same time the possibility of not doing it. But if to be human is also to be conscious, then I am always keenly aware of the possibility of either committing or not committing a certain act. Anguish is awareness of myself as possibility. In anguish I am apprehensive not of the external world, but of what I might do or not do (". . . it is the very being of horror to appear to itself as 'not being the cause' of the conduct it calls for"). I may, for example, walk out in front of an oncoming car or, despite my resolutions to be courageous, prove to be a coward in battle.

This self-distrust, this hiatus between the ideal and the actual, is for Sartre inevitable in human reality and constitutes the basis for human value. Since Nothingness separates man from his ideal, he is tempted to "fill" that gap with himself. He would become his ideal, make it part of him (*appropriate* it), as if it were a meal that he was ingesting. But as a for-itself, he can never *be* the ideal he has set up for himself. Consciousness can never effect a *unity*

---

[5] Neither in *Being and Nothingness* nor in his subsequent writings does Sartre reject psychoanalysis as such. He takes issue only with certain aspects of Freud's method, such as the equivocal function of the *censor* (which hides from itself what it already "knows") or the existence in the psyche of primal, archetypal complexes to which all later experience in an individual's life can be reduced. However, Sartre does lay more stress today on the effect of external circumstances on our lives (*la force des choses* or *being-in-the-world*). He now admits that we are "conditioned" by historical and social forces. But his commitment to Marxism is anything but passive. Nor does he see any contradiction between conditioning and freedom. Man is free not only to change the society that helped form him, but also to determine the manner in which he will respond to that conditioning (which is always external to him) and to decide what life he will lead. As recently as 1970, Sartre said: "For the idea that I have never ceased to develop is that in the end one is always responsible for what is made of one. Even if one can do nothing else besides assume this responsibility. For I believe that a man can always make something out of what is made of him. This is the limit I would today accord to freedom: the small movement which makes of a totally conditioned social being someone who does not render back completely what his conditioning has given him. Which makes of Genet a poet when he had been rigorously conditioned to be a thief." ("An Interview with Sartre," first published in *New Left Review*, No. 58, reprinted in *The New York Review of Books*, XIV, Number 6, March 26, 1970, pp. 22-31.)

with its object; it can only be in a dynamic *relationship* with it. I may proceed *as if* I were my ideal, vigilantly reminding myself that I can never *in fact* be it, and therefore be *authentic*; or I can attempt to conceal from myself the basic truth that we can never *be* our ideal and, consequently, act in *bad faith.*[6]

Bad faith invariably involves the attempt to escape the freedom of the for-itself and take refuge in the snug causality that governs a thing (in-itself). In fleeting moments we catch ourselves up in this game, but the passive inertness of an object is so comfortable, and the anguish of freedom so painful, that we are tempted to "put the truth out of mind." Nonetheless, since to be human is to be conscious, we can at best only turn our attention away from what we know we are doing. In other words, we lie to ourselves, for we know we are vacillating between two irreconcilable modes of being. Sartre cites the example of a girl out on a date with a man who she knows wishes to seduce her but who she pretends (to herself as well as him) has no such intention. She knows that the flattering words he speaks and the gestures he makes have as their ultimate purpose taking her to bed; yet she cuts them off from their intention and responds to them as if they were only what they appeared to be. When he takes her hand into his, she leaves it there as if it were a disembodied thing for which she has no responsibility, despite the fact that in another part of her mind she knows his holding her hand is just one more step leading to the ultimate decision she will have to make. She plays as if she were a thing, yet she knows she is not one. Her excitement, in fact, springs out of this dialectic between her awareness of her freedom and her temporary renunciation of it:

> This is because she does not quite know what she wants. She is profoundly aware of the desire which she inspires, but the desire cruel and naked would humiliate and horrify her. Yet she would find no charm in a respect which would be only respect. In order to satisfy her, there must be a feeling which is addressed *wholly* to her *personality*—i.e., to her full freedom—and which would be a recognition of her freedom. But at the same time this feeling must be wholly desire, it must address itself to her body as object.

---

[6] Bad faith is exemplified in the "coward" and the "stinker" (*salaud*): "Those who hide their complete freedom from themselves out of a spirit of seriousness or by means of deterministic excuses, I shall call cowards; those who try to show that their existence was necessary, when it is the very contingency of man's appearance on earth, I shall call stinkers."

The young woman's bad faith does not consist in her misleading the man. (Lying to others is not necessarily bad faith.) It resides in her identification with a fixed role which she simultaneously rejects: "... the ambiguity necessary for bad faith comes from the fact that I affirm here that *I am* my own transcendence in the mode of being a thing" [that is, I attempt to deny my own reality and become a thing].

Bad faith is not merely a question of hypocrisy. Even when we are "sincere" we are in bad faith. Sincerity is the conviction that we *are* what we claim to be. But the claim automatically denies the identification: a slither of Nothingness insinuates itself between what we are and what we would be. For if the two were one, we would never be conscious of a division. Humans, unlike animals, are *self*-conscious. No matter how earnestly they try to adapt their actions to their words they can never be identical with their conception of themselves because consciousness is always consciousness of *not* being the object it posits for itself (here the image of "self"). Sartre's equation of sincerity with bad faith does not mean that he denies ideals or values. On the contrary, to be free is to choose and all choice presupposes value. But value is always a possibility, a project belonging to the future. Even if, for example, I have demonstrated by my actions that "I am a courageous man," those actions belong to my past and I must continually renew my ideal of a courageous man. Yet no sooner do I "realize" it than it slips into the past and I must project myself toward it once more, ad infinitum.

I never *am* a courageous man, or anything else, because man in contrast to being-in-itself never *is* but is always *becoming*. His being is "what it is not" and "not what it is." We are not our past, though we may say it is a "part" of us or, more strictly, "belongs" to us like a thing, fixed, finished and complete (in-itself). In fact, we are perpetually moving away from the past even as we are "creating" it; only with our deaths does it catch up to us, at which point consciousness ceases and we become one with pure being-in-itself. Thus man *is not* (now) what he *is* (his past). Man *is,* instead, his future, in the sense that the future is a plan, a model, an ideal freely chosen, of what he would be. But the future *is not* yet; it is only possibility; it cannot *be* (in the sense of being-in-itself) until our death, at which point it will cease to be the future. Thus man is (now) what he is not (his future). *"I am the self which I will be, in the mode of not being it"* [italics Sartre's]. In flight from his past, which is fixed and definite; forever reaching for the future, which can never be, man is suspended in the tension of the present contemplating his Nothingness *vis-à-vis* being-in-itself. To deny this equilibrium is to be in bad faith.

Another area in which we commonly exhibit bad faith is in our relations to other people (the Other). Human reality is social; though each of us experiences the world as if it "belonged" to him, he cannot escape the Other. Thus as I view the world as mine, the Other sees it as his. His perspective, or *gaze,* is an intrusion into my world. A disruption takes place. My subjectivity is confronted by the subjectivity of the Other, and the structure and meaning I have given to things is challenged by a new organization. Furthermore, in his gaze I experience *shame.* For it impales me as if I were a passive thing, strips me of the meaning I give myself and incorporates me into the Other's "universe."[7]

To hold my own against the Other, I can play the role of object (being-for-others) or subject (being-for-myself). As object, I can attempt to dominate him by making him dependent on me-as-object: I can make myself pleasing to him (*pride*) or submissive or *masochistic.* Or I can return his gaze and become a subject again who attempts to reduce him to an object. Then I can become *indifferent* to him (allow my look to pass over him as if he were an insignificant thing) or *sadistic* (derive my pleasure from the pain I inflict on him). This tug-of-war is most blatant in the relationship between man and woman, particularly in sex. In coition the man and the woman attempt to suspend consciousness and become pure flesh (*incarnation*) in order to appropriate one another's subjectivity. Man attempts to *be* penis, woman attempts to *be* vagina. The man-penis would fill the woman-hole with being. But the hole only seems to be passive; like the penis, it is personified consciousness in quest of power:

> The obscenity of the feminine sex is that of everything which "gapes open." It is an *appeal to being* as all holes are. In herself woman appeals to a strange flesh which is to transform her into a fullness of being by penetration and dissolution. Conversely woman senses her condition as an appeal precisely because she is "in the form of a hole." This is the true origin of Adler's complex. Beyond any doubt her sex is a mouth and a voracious mouth which devours the penis—a fact which can easily lead to the idea of castration.

In all of these relationships each partner acts in bad faith, whether he attempts to make of the Other, or become himself, an object. The cardinal lie consists in the fact that they are both well aware of the humanness (for-itself) of one another in the very moment that they attempt to

---

[7] The character Garcin in *No Exit* points up the moral of the play with the line, "Hell is—other people."

become a thing (in-itself) or reduce the Other to one. In fact, Sartre points out, the desire to possess a person differs from the desire to possess a thing in that we wish to appropriate the person with his freedom intact. (The lover is bored with a totally submissive mistress; the sadist's pleasure ends, and with it his sadism, when the victim ceases to squirm.) Clearly, it is impossible for one person to possess (*appropriate*) another. Man is distinct from a thing precisely insofar as he has freedom, which can neither be relinquished nor destroyed. As Sartre's own experience as a prisoner of war testifies, the torturer can always read a "No" in the eyes of his victim even after he has beaten it off his lips. Therefore, love, sadism, masochism, seduction, pride, indifference—all the twisted forms that human relations can assume—are false and are doomed to failure.[8]

If we push Sartre's notion of bad faith to its extreme, we must conclude that man seeks to be God. Of course Sartre rejects a literal God, if we are to understand God to be an omnipotent creator who is at one with his creation. (If God is the Creator of Being, then what is God's relation to Being? What is the origin of God? What *is* God?) Yet the idea of God, despite its inherent contradiction, is the ideal that man seeks to be. Man would like to have the unrestricted freedom of the Creator (for-itself) combined with God's omnipotence and total self-sufficiency (in-itself). Man, in other words, seeks to be for-itself-in-itself. He seeks total Being as well as total freedom. But since freedom by definition is non-Being, he acts in bad faith. For in his freedom, he would deny his freedom. Man, in this mode of Being, is futile:

> Thus the passion of man is the reverse of that of Christ, for man loses himself as man in order that God may be born. But the idea of God is contradictory and we lose ourselves in vain. Man is a useless passion.

But Sartre goes on to qualify this statement, specifying that man is a "useless passion" only if he acts in bad faith. Man is also capable of *authenticity,* which is the honest acknowledgement of his total freedom. In anguish the authentic man recognizes himself as forever striving for the

---

[8] Of course Sartre acknowledges, even in *Being and Nothingness,* the possibility of men working together for some common end. In this case, individuals form a group and direct their collective gaze on something or somebody outside of the group. But this temporary alliance, says Sartre, can never bridge the inevitable gap between members within the group. As individuals in relation to one another, they still function according to the subject/object dichotomy and can never merge their separate subjectivities to form a true brotherhood (*Mit-sein*).

self-sufficiency of being-in-itself yet knows he can never achieve it. The man of bad faith is a "failure" not because he fails to achieve Being, but because he refuses to accept himself as non-Being. Sinking into despair only compounds his bad faith. The authentic man, on the other hand, does not shirk action (he knows he cannot *not* act, that even "withdrawal" is action), nor does he "rest" on his laurels (like Goethe's Faust, who, upon completing the major work of his life, exclaims, "Ah, stay the moment!"). Man is not any one of his acts; he is the ensemble of his actions, which can be toted up only with his death. Therefore, if freedom imposes responsibility on man, it also offers him possibility (Sartre calls his philosophy an "optimistic toughness"). Man is not bound by his past failures, just as he is not determined by his physical handicap. The future is wide open because he *is* not.

Yet what consolation can we draw from a philosophy that assures us freedom but withholds from us any inducement to use it (other than that we have to)? What is conspicuously lacking in Sartre's system is justification and motivation for action. Values, as we have seen, are only provisional: they must constantly be reaffirmed or supplanted by new ones. But since Sartre rejects a first cause (or universal essence) for man, one value is as "right" as the next one provided only that we act (*value* and *action* are actually synonymous). We are thus back with Dostoevsky's problem in *Notes from Underground*: if God is dead then everything is permissible. Sartre is even more austere than his predecessor. Dostoevsky, at least, admitted the possibility of contentment for Chernyshevsky's Utilitarian materialist, even though he had contempt for him. Sartre, like the dour prophet of *Ecclesiastes,* must condemn as vain aspirations to such fundamental human conditions as self-fulfillment, security or happiness. For each of these conditions presupposes a finality—a stasis or pause, however brief—in which man attempts to arrest the fleeting present in order to savor his good fortune. And even if he could hold back the onrush of time, when he contemplates (i.e., *appropriates*) the cause of his satisfaction, he has lost it. For Sartre, as for the Buddhist, appropriation is impossible because the essence of man is Nothingness: non-Being always intrudes itself between man and the world. But while the Buddhist harangues only against worldly possession (*samsara*), the Nothingness he seeks is actually oneness with being-in-itself, and whether we call his escape from samsara *nirvana* or *possession* of Being, the distinction is only semantic; for atheistic Sartre, on the other hand, Nothingness is only too literal.

In cutting man off from Being (in-itself), Sartre isolates him in a subjective cell. We have already considered the futility of human intercourse, in which the Other can never be "thou" but only "it." But Sartrean man is also severed from his own ego. Since at any given moment it belongs to our past, it is always outside of us, and consciousness can no more apprehend the ego than it can any other external object. Thus just as the sexual act is a futile attempt to penetrate "into" the Other's subjectivity, so self-identification is a useless attempt to get into ourselves. Finally, Sartre alienates man from nature, the body, matter in general. He describes nature and the material world as he would a colossal vagina. It is slimy, oozy, clammy, viscous and dense. We fear it, for it would devour us as the female sex organ would the penis.

Cut off from God, society and nature; a stranger to himself and his past; committed to a future which forever eludes him, Sartre's Existentialist is little more than a succession of hard, steely pinpoints of freedom vainly filling up the holes in Being which he himself has punctured. He can despair and voluntarily renounce life or retreat into some underground hole. Or he can project himself into some enterprise to which he attaches value, however provisional, and thus transcend underground man. In any event, he will retain the latter's lucidity and not, like the bourgeois *salaud,* seek ultimate justification for what he does.

In his fictional and dramatic works, Sartre invariably depicts an individual caught up in a situation that demands a crucial and, frequently, immediate decision. Occasionally the course of action is clear, particularly for characters who are monolithically dedicated to some cause, e.g., the Communists Brunet in *The Ways of Liberty* and Canoris in *Death Without Burial*. More often, the protagonist is in a dilemma, wavering between several alternatives. He may, like Mathieu in *The Age of Reason* (the first volume of *The Ways of Liberty*), simply avoid making a decision, then find that he must pay the consequences for his "inaction" nonetheless; or he might, like Mathieu in *Troubled Sleep* (the third volume) act "absurdly," that is, from sheer frustration and the long-suppressed need to initiate action rather than from any rational calculation of ends and means. *Nausea,* which precedes by several years the publication of *Being and Nothingness,* focuses more on the conditions leading up to the final decision than on the decision itself; yet the resolution of that novel consists of a choice which will presumably change the protagonist's life and thus deliver him from underground.

NAUSEA

When we consider the power of *Nausea,* we are struck by its seeming uneventfulness. The "action" can be summed up in a few words. The protagonist, Antoine Roquentin, is writing a biography of an historical figure, the Marquis de Rollebon. In attempting to reconstruct the Marquis' life, he comes to the realization that he cannot even give form to his own life, nor, for that matter, to any other real thing. Consequently, he gives up working on the biography and decides to write a fictional work, perhaps a novel. But these events are only the surface bobbings of Sartre's real subject, which is no less than the metaphysical problem of Being (both in-itself and for-itself). *Nausea,* then, is the dramatic representation of what happens to a man when he discovers, in horror and "nausea," the reality of being-in-itself, his own connection with it as for-itself (*facticity*), and the options that are open to him. It is, in fact, the literary forerunner of the epic system formulated in *Being and Nothingness.* The abstractions of the later work are concretely portrayed in the novel, which, written in the form of the diary, pulls us into the hero's unique, subjective confrontation with Being.

Sartre must make credible in the novel what is only assumed in the philosophical tome, namely, the actual process by which any given individual comes to concern himself with being-in-itself (or *existence,* as Sartre calls it in the novel). For the average reader questions about the ultimate nature of reality are probably academic. For underground Roquentin, on the other hand, they are an obsession: at times he is literally overwhelmed by existence. Whether Roquentin can be called an Existentialist remains to be seen. But the fact is that his perceptiveness, sensitivity and ruthless intellectual honesty, along with his precarious isolation and freedom, make him especially susceptible to Sartre's Existentialism and thus lend it credibility.

Like Steppenwolf and Underground Man, Roquentin suffers from too much freedom. When the novel opens his single commitment is to the biography of the Marquis. He has already amassed considerable data on his subject and is completing his research in the municipal library of Bouville (presumably Le Havre, France). But the more he ponders his subject, the more elusive it becomes. His problem is not simply whether all of his data are accurate. Even if he could be certain of his "facts," how he puts them together must ultimately be arbitrary. What he discovers is that he can never "know" the real Rollebon (as he can, say, an object under a microscope) and that all biographies have something of the biographer in them:

> Not a glimmer comes from Rollebon's side. Slow, lazy, sulky, the facts adapt themselves to the rigour of the order I wish to give them; but it remains outside of them. I have the feeling of doing a work of pure imagination.[9]

Roquentin's objections to the writing of biography are, of course, specious. The biographer should be fully aware that, like the novelist, he can only interpret, or "reconstruct," his subject and should therefore not aspire to create a perfect likeness of it.[10] The fact is that Roquentin is bored with his work. He suddenly comes to the realization that he has been attempting to give his own life meaning by resuscitating an insignificant marquis who has been dead for over a century: the biography, and only it, is his reason for being. He has also been undergoing a crisis concerning his own past, which he is finding increasingly difficult to grasp. When he looks back upon it, he can see only an uninterrupted flow of "events," one merging imperceptibly with the other and lacking a clearly delineated beginning, middle or end. It is only when he talks about the past, in retrospect, that it assumes a definitive form, which like biography distorts the actual experience. If, then, Roquentin cannot believe in his own past, how can he presume to write a biography about Rollebon? He concludes that the past, both his and Rollebon's, might just as well be dead:

> The true nature of the present revealed itself: it was what exists, and all that was not present did not exist. The past did not exist. . . . For me the past was only a pensioning off: it was another way of existing, a state of vacation and inaction; each event, when it had played its part, put itself politely into a box and became an honorary event: we have so much difficulty imagining nothingness.

But in discarding the biography of the Marquis, Roquentin renounces his only real involvement in the present. What follows is an unremitting, at

[9]Jean-Paul Sartre, *Nausea,* tr. Lloyd Alexander, New York, 1959. Subsequent quotations from *Nausea* are from this edition.
[10]If Sartre ever shared Roquentin's aversion to biography, he has certainly had a change of heart in recent years. Consider, for example, the prodigious efforts he has devoted to Genet, Baudelaire and Flaubert.

times excruciating, *ennui*. Not the least of Sartre's achievements in *Nausea*
is his vivid depiction of the slow, lumbering movement of Roquentin's
day, with each moment hanging heavily and each of the pauses between
events stretching into its own eternity. Roquentin must find things to do
simply to get through the day. Hence throughout most of the novel he sits
in the park, the library, or various cafes idly watching people; or he drifts in
and out of museums and other public places, reading inscriptions on
statues that nobody else bothers to read; or he explores the city, less out of
curiosity than out of a need to be moving. He might as well be a
free-floating molecule. Nothing he does is necessary: whether he should
rouse himself in the morning or dawdle in bed, read a book or go to a
movie, can be decided by the flip of a coin. Yet these actions, however
trivial, are the only proof that he is alive; they alone distinguish him from
an inanimate object, which he sees himself rapidly becoming. With
Steppenwolf and Underground Man, Roquentin feels all the anguish of
freedom without the solace of purpose.

It is only natural that his disengagement from life in general should
include dissociation from other people. Since he is a newcomer to Bouville,
his social contacts are scarcely more intimate than those of the solitary
tourist passing through a foreign city. They consist of brief exchanges with
waitresses and other service people, an occasional conversation (but always
impersonal on Roquentin's part) with a casual acquaintance he has met in
the library, and a purely sexual relationship with a slovenly cafe proprietress
(with fat hands), who requires sex at least once a day with whomever is
available and who often does not even bother to remove her clothes.
Generally, however, Sartre depicts Roquentin as being essentially alone.
Moreover, his solitude is intensified by the fact that other people are usually
in clusters, such as a family taking a walk, a couple on a date, a group of
diners or cardplayers, children at play, and the like.

Roquentin's radical alienation from people, while aggravated by his
being a stranger in the town, is ultimately metaphysical in origin. Other
people for him are the Other of *Being and Nothingness*. They subject him to
their gaze, he returns it; and both experience *shame* as the one attempts to
reduce the other to an object. But since Roquentin's Other is generally a
group, he, at least in the beginning of the novel, is at a disadvantage. To
Roquentin, who stands apart from it, the group is a single unit, an
ensemble, whose power is compounded by its numbers. Members of the
group reflect back to each other an image which defines them and which
they attempt to live up to: by mutually restricting their freedom they assign

each other a distinct being and place in the universe. Roquentin, on the other hand, has no such support. Hence his isolation only adds to his anxiety and his growing conviction that he is not human:

> Or perhaps it is because I am a single man? People who live in society have learned how to see themselves in mirrors as they appear to their friends. I have no friends. Is that why my flesh is so naked? You might say—yes you might say, nature without humanity.

As Sartre points out in *Being and Nothingness,* our being-for-others takes for granted a reason, or "justification," for our existence: our Being becomes what others demand, or what we think they demand, of us. This, of course, is in bad faith, since man by nature (for-itself) is a Nothingness and, therefore, without cause or purpose (*de trop*). But until Requentin comes to recognize the bad faith of the middle-class townsfolk, they succeed in intimidating him. They make him feel ashamed of his isolation, as if he were a Steppenwolf or Underground Man stumbling into their Sunday parlor, or a humorless man who scared children away. He even feels the reproachful eye of the Bouvillan dead on him. In one of the most brilliant scenes in the novel, Roquentin in the art museum is viewing a series of paintings of the city's founding fathers—soldiers, statesmen, businessmen, jurists—all executed on commission by the town's official portraitist. As if he had used Rembrandt's *Syndics* as his model, the artist has bestowed on them the dignity and stature befitting their station. Roquentin is struck by their apparent self-possession, their seemingly unfaltering conviction that they have discharged their duty to God, country and family, and that the life they have led so exemplarly is the only life in this best of possible worlds. Each portrait is a mute judgment of him, and his inevitable punishment is allegorized in a singular painting called *The Death of the Bachelor,* depicting the dead man in his bed and, in the background, his false mistress and her real lover ransacking the bureau containing the deceased's money. All of the paintings make Roquentin feel guilty, but the look of one dignitary in particular spotlights him in his underground: ". . . his judgment went right through me like a sword and questioned my very right to exist. And it was true. . . ."

Since Roquentin is generally at a distance from people, he can only imagine their relations with one another. Yet he suspects that as he is separated from them as a group, so they are isolated from each other as individuals within the group. Sartre tells us in *Being and Nothingness*:

> It is therefore useless for human-reality to seek to get out of this
> dilemma: one must either transcend the Other or allow oneself to be
> transcended by him. The essence of the relations between conscious-
> nesses is . . . conflict.

Thus Roquentin deduces from the concierge's complaints that her al-
coholic husband abuses her (sadism) and that she seems to thrive on the
abuse (masochism); or, from overhearing a conversation between a couple
in the restaurant, that they will make love that afternoon (incarnation) even
though the girl, like the coquette in *Being and Nothingness,* affects ignorance
of her and her boyfriend's real intention (bad faith). But inasmuch as the
novel is told in the first person, it is Roquentin's own rare encounters with
individuals that most graphically illustrate the inevitable failure of human
relations. Mention has already been made of the purely sexual affair with
the proprietress, in which neither she nor Roquentin pretend to be
anything more than animated flesh giving and receiving pleasure. More
complex relations are his attempted rapport with a Mr. Ogier P. . . (the
Self-Taught Man) and with Roquentin's former mistress, Anny.

The Self-Taught Man is a solitary, unprepossessing middle-aged
bachelor who spends most of his free time reading in the library. Like
Roquentin, he is a marginal person, unobtrusive and of uncertain origin.
He is also under suspicion, later justified, of being a homosexual. Roquentin has mixed feelings about him. On the one hand, he feels aversion. For if
the solid citizens reinforce each other's sense of belonging, pariahs such as
the Self-Taught Man reflect back to Roquentin his own insignificance,
superfluousness and dubious identity. On the other hand, he feels compassion for him: Roquentin knows only too well the Self-Taught Man's
alienation and, hence, sadness. Even though Roquentin can barely tolerate
him, he is friendly to him. Like Underground Man, whose loneliness drove
him to visit people he actually loathed, Roquentin has a basic need for
human companionship.

It takes only a couple of conversations, however, for Roquentin to regret
having made overtures to the bookish clerk. The Self-Taught Man is
actually a *salaud* who takes his measure of values unquestioningly from a
source outside of himself. Despite his alienation, it never occurs to him that
there is any difference between himself and the bourgeois townsfolk. He is,
in fact, their dupe, paying homage to their culture at the same time that he
is excluded from it. For example, he is determined to read every book in the
local library (in alphabetical order!), taking what he reads at face value. In
the same uncritical spirit, he has adopted socialism and a fuzzy humanism.

He exclaims to Roquentin at one point, "there is a goal, Monsieur, there is a goal . . . there is humanity." Having rejected God, he has taken for his motto: Whatever is human is good. But his humanism, like his reading, is untested and therefore unreal and sentimental. He has neither thought it through nor made it an active principle of conduct. Actually, the real basis for his love of mankind is a concrete, physical desire for individual men, which he does not admit to himself, even when he is caught red-handed stroking the hand of a teen-age boy in full view of the horrified occupants of the library.

Roquentin (and presumably the young Sartre) are bitterly critical of the Self-Taught Man's humanism. They see it as an amorphous doctrine swallowing up, digesting and reducing to placid homogeneity the diversity in human beings:

> . . . the humanist philosopher who bends over his brothers like a wise elder brother who has a sense of his responsibilities; the humanist who loves men as they are, the humanist who loves men as they ought to be, the one who wants to save them with their consent and the one who will save them in spite of themselves, the one who wants to create new myths, and the one who is satisfied with the old ones, the one who loves death in man, the one who loves life in man, the happy humanist who always has the right word to make people laugh, the sober humanist whom you meet especially at funerals or wakes. They all hate each other: as individuals, naturally not as men. But the Self-Taught Man doesn't know it: he has locked them up inside himself like cats in a bag and they are tearing each other in pieces without his noticing it.[11]

Not only does the Self-Taught Man's humanism belie our inescapable individuality (hence isolation), but it offers only a deceptive refuge, a static in-itself which we can only embrace in bad faith. Roquentin is particularly

---

[11] In *Existentialism and Human Emotions,* Sartre is careful to distinguish between two meanings of the term *humanism.* Humanism, as it applies to the Self-Taught Man, is simply the substitution of one absolute, man, for another, God. This, of course, is directly contradictory to Sartre's Existentialism, since it postulates a universal human ideal (essence) existing prior to individual men (existants), thus reversing the cardinal principle of Sartre's ethics, namely existence precedes essence. Moreover, it provides a given ideal for all men; whereas for the Existentialist, value is never given in advance and each man makes his own. Humanism in the second sense of the word implies that man invents his own values rather than receiving them from someone outside of him (e.g., God), and that reality is always a human reality. It is the latter meaning that Sartre has in mind when he describes his own philosophy as *humanistic.*

offended at this point because he has been stripping himself of his own comfortable lies and defenses. It is precisely his acceptance of his own Nothingness that has brought him to the point of near despair. Thus the ironic advocacy of togetherness by the lonely Self-Taught Man, rather than alleviating, actually underscores Roquentin's isolation.

Roquentin is skeptical of human relations. However, his loneliness is so overpowering that he makes a last, desperate effort to revive his friendship with Anny, his former mistress, even after he has come to the conclusion that his past is dead. Within minutes after seeing her again, he realizes that he is pursuing ghosts.

Nowhere in all of Sartre's fiction do we find so stark a portrait of what is, apparently, an inevitable, an ontological, alienation between people.[12] Love is totally lacking between these former "lovers," who come to each other exclusively for their own needs. Roquentin seeks in Anny the kind of human support which the townsfolk provide one another. He feels that she alone can provide him substance and identity. He would like her, in particular, to reflect back to him an image of the new Roquentin, one who has experienced some profound change of which she would approve. Instead, she sees him as she always has, as a bungling, unimaginative, do-nothing intellectual who is not even good in bed. She refuses to see the change which, in fact, has occurred in him, because it is a threat which would disrupt her subjective conception of their relationship. She prefers him fixed, like a thing, a stage property having a preassigned function within a scene of her own making. Moreover, only a static Roquentin would enable her to mark more clearly her own change. Hence Anny and Roquentin are at an impasse, speaking at cross-purposes, trapped in private worlds into which they vainly attempt to assimilate one another.

The tension between them is also Sartre's earliest and most vivid fictional depiction of the war between the sexes. While the male is frequently the dominant figure in Sartre's love games (e.g., Brunet in *The Ways of Liberty*), Roquentin is no match for Anny. Again, the reader would have to turn to Sartre's drama (to the lesbian Inez in *No Exit*) to find as consummate a bitch as the young and possibly misogynous Sartre has created in Anny. Hard and cynical—she says she is dead—she has, like Roquentin, reached the point where there are no more adventures (she calls them "perfect moments"). Arbitrary and unpredictable, she openly shows contempt for him, frequently calling him stupid when he fails to read her thoughts,

---

[12] It is matched only by the situation of the three damned souls in Sartre's play, *No Exit*.

deliberately making him uneasy then standing back to enjoy his discomfort. Repeatedly she subjects him to her gaze, before which he is considerably more uncomfortable than when he stood before the portraits of Bouville's founding fathers.

Yet Roquentin, not ordinarily a weak man, is a willing pawn to her sadism. Masochist he will be if only he can lay hold of (possess) the person of Anny. He is thus acting in bad faith. Like the townsfolk and the Self-Taught Man, who relinquish their freedom in order to merge respectively with the community and with humanity, Roquentin invites Anny's domination over him in order to become one with her. In the past Anny connived at his self-deception, for in her attempt to possess him she too was acting in bad faith. Now she has tired of the game. On her part, the "love" has all but disappeared from their love-hate relationship of the past, and the manipulation of Roquentin's freedom no longer interests her. With her curt dismissal of him ("Get out!"), Roquentin knows what he preferred not to know—he cannot escape his freedom.

Thus Sartre's underground man is without the help of other people; he is not engaged in any meaningful activity; he is without hope, purpose or conviction of any kind. He sees himself as something not quite human:

> . . . I hadn't the right to exist. I had appeared by chance, I existed like a stone, a plant or a microbe. My life put out feelers towards small pleasures in every direction. Sometimes it sent out vague signals; at other times I felt nothing more than a harmless buzzing.

At the same time, however, he retains his human consciousness and his overwrought sensibility. Stripped of the supports by which men ordinarily keep their footing, he feels raw and exposed and falls victim to a paralyzing anxiety. He is alienated from the world, and it in turn becomes strange to him. Little by little he begins to doubt the most elementary "certainties," as he gradually becomes aware of being-in-itself, or existence.

What Sartre describes in the cold and precise language of the philosopher in *Being and Nothingness* takes on, in the novel, a nightmarish vividness. Roquentin is certainly not mad. Yet he perceives, as if in an hallucinatory state, the flux and formlessness of matter. He experiences the world apart from the usual categories around which the mind organizes it, such as time, place, function, measure, relationship and the like; he sees these categories for what they are, abstractions, while the things themselves ". . . are divorced from their names." Objects seem ready to move from their customary place, like an invading army, before which Roquentin, who is "in the way," shudders in dread. Or they lose their individual shape, color and texture as they melt into a grotesque, sticky mass, like molten lava or paste. Existence pulsates, threatens each moment to burst. It is unpredictable (the "laws" of nature are an illusion). It is abundant, overflowing, superfluous (*de trop*):

> Existence everywhere, infinitely, in excess, for ever and everywhere; existence—which is limited only by existence. I sat down on the bench, stupefied, stunned by this profusion of beings without origin: everywhere blossomings, hatchings out, my ears buzzed with existence, my very flesh throbbed and opened, abandoned itself to the universal burgeoning. It was repugnant.

In the beginning Roquentin gets the urge to literally flee whenever he feels this repugnance, or nausea:

> We were a heap of living creatures, irritated, embarrassed at ourselves, we hadn't the slightest reason to be there, none of us, each one, confused, vaguely alarmed, felt in the way in relation to the others. *In the way.* . . .

But it is not long before he realizes that there is nowhere to run, since existence is everywhere. Indeed, his most traumatic discovery is that he himself exists, as well as Anny, the Self-Taught Man, the citizens of Bouville, and the whole human race. People and objects lose their characteristic distinctions: objects are animated, and people are imperfect syntheses whose parts have an independent will of their own, such as the Self-Taught Man's hand, which reaches over to stroke the hand of the boy sitting next to him, as if the two hands were autonomous entities severed from their respective bodies. In *Being and Nothingness* Sartre defines nausea as the "taste" of one's "facticity," that is, his awareness of the link, through his body, between "himself" and pure being. In his worst moments Roquentin gags on existence—he would like to vomit it out. (". . . I'm suffocating: existence penetrates me everywhere, through the eyes, the nose, the mouth.") As being overwhelms him, he loses his fundamental orientation to the earth, as if he were caught in a maelstrom or were spinning around the room in a state of acute inebriation. In his impotence, he despairs of freedom:

There were those idiots who came to tell you about will power and struggle for life. Hadn't they ever seen a beast or a tree?

Even his thought processes get caught up in the relentless vortex of Being. He cannot control them. Like a phrase or melody that persists in our mind in spite of our efforts to suppress it, his thoughts go their independent way in maddening circularity. Descartes' "I think, therefore I am," from which Sartre's entire metaphysics seems to have sprung, becomes a hall of cracked mirrors in Roquentin's mind:

> I am. I am, I exist, I think, therefore I am; I am because I think, why
> do I think? I don't want to think any more, I am because I think that
> I don't want to be, I think that I . . . because . . . ugh! I flee.

Consciousness, like being-in-itself, seems to have no definitive beginning or end here. In fact, it becomes indistinguishable from Being.

Roquentin's new awareness of existence has at least one compensation: it clears the air. Henceforth, he need not be intimidated by the Bouvillan bourgeoisie, for example, for they too are prey to existence. He knows that it lurks beneath the flattering brushstrokes of the portraits hanging in the municipal gallery, and that the artist only distorted nature to make his subjects look more impressive. *Nausea,* like *Notes from Underground,* is a philosophical novel dealing with a reality common to all men. It is therefore a mistake to read it simply, or primarily, as a clinical study of an individual neurosis. Yet the experience of Roquentin, if not the man himself, often borders on the pathological. His reaction to Being has the structure of a mental breakdown. Although all men are encompassed by Being, and some are aware of the fact, they do not necessarily allow themselves to be overpowered by it.

If existence "bursts" through the categories in which he customarily perceives it, Roquentin is still responsible for both the categories and their subsequent absence. For example, being-in-itself does not "move." Neither is it "fixed." These are relative terms, one dependent on the other, which human consciousness imposes on absolute Being. Roquentin is like the young lover who projects an image on his mistress and then is distressed when she does not conform to it. What Roquentin fails to realize is the mind's unique capacity for *nihilating withdrawal.* If man is "that being which is its own Nothingness" (who can conceive of absence, destruction, negation, and so forth), then by definition he cannot be swallowed up by Being. Consciousness can stand apart from Being—indeed, it can even stand back from itself, thus invalidating the tortuous vicious circle of Descartes' *I think, therefore I am.*[13]

But Roquentin can do more than merely keep existence at bay. He can interact with Being, as if it were a sparring partner to help keep him in shape, or a lump of clay on which he might carve an image of himself. To be sure, the form and meaning that he might "give" to Being could only be relative and subjective—Being is what it *is* and cannot literally change. Nonetheless, he is free to act. Indeed, his refusal to be active in relation to Being is itself an action, a free choice. Therefore, his denial of free will is a more blatant example of bad faith than that of the townsfolk. For if these people erroneously assign an ultimate purpose to their actions (the meaning of which is derived from an external source), they, at least, are engaged (*engagé*) in the business of life and acknowledge their engagement. Roquentin, on the other hand, chooses to be passive and then bemoans the fact that he cannot dissociate himself from inorganic matter.

Throughout the novel Roquentin, like Underground Man and Steppenwolf, has had many glimmers of his need to act. He has observed that, in some of his worst moments of panic, he had only to make some positive effort for his self-assurance to return, such as returning the gaze of some hostile townsman, writing in his journal, standing firm instead of fleeing during his attacks of nausea. Repeatedly he has regretted his "wasted days"; Anny and the Self-Taught Man reproach him for his inactivity. Ironically, as critical as Sartre is of Self-Taught Man's fuzzy humanism, he puts in his mouth the words that are later to become the cornerstone of Sartre's Existentialist ethic:

> ... voluntary optimism. Life has a meaning if we choose to give it one. One must first act, throw one's self into some enterprise. Then, if one reflects, the die is already cast.

---

[13] In *Being and Nothingness,* Sartre postulates two modes of consciousness, *reflective* and *prereflective.* Prereflective consciousness is primal, one might almost say instinctual. It is concommitant with existence. Reflective consciousness occurs after (and reflects on) prereflective consciousness. Roquentin's ability to think about himself is not the cause of his existence: he exists first and then thinks about his existence. Reflective consciousness can only affirm existence by contemplating the existential fact of the prereflective consciousness. Prereflective consciousness can only affirm (or deny) something other than itself. Thus, for Sartre, Descartes logically infers his existence from his consciousness (reflective) of his consciousness (prereflective).

Roquentin only scoffed at this suggestion when the Self-Taught Man made it. He had not yet undergone that swift succession of crises that we have just examined: his loss of interest in the biography, Anny's final rejection, and, of course, his traumatic discovery of the nature of existence. He had yet to experience the anguish and desperation of discovering his own Nothingness and, like Sartre's models, René Descartes, to strip himself of everything but his doubt.

At the very conclusion of *Nausea,* Roquentin does finally commit himself to a definitive course of action: he decides to write a novel. Sartre's one-page resolution to *Nausea* has struck many readers as both anticlimactic and incommensurate with the problem that it is supposed to resolve. It suggests that if he were not actually indifferent to Roquentin's "solution," he was certainly less concerned with it than he was with the painful process by which Roquentin arrives at it. We need not concern ourselves with the artistic merit of the ending, but we should at least attempt to explain this process.

Roquentin's recourse to art is suggested to him while he listens, for the last time, to the jazz record, "Some of these days, you'll miss me honey." During his most acute attacks of nausea, he was always able to find relief in the song. For the song, and by implication all art, has precisely those properties that Roquentin despairs of finding in actual objects (existants). Art has form. It is precise and rigorous. It has an "internal necessity," by means of which it retains its identity when everything else changes. And though we experience it through the world of matter, it is beyond existence, like Plato's Ideas:

> You can't say it exists. The turning record exists, the air struck by the
> voice which vibrates, exists, the voice which made an impression on
> the record existed. I who listen, I exist. All is full, existence
> everywhere, dense, heavy and sweet. But, beyond all this sweetness,
> inaccessible, near and so far, young, merciless and serene, there is this
> ... this rigour.

Hesitantly, still quite unsure of himself, he resolves that he too will create something. Since his talent lies in writing, it would have to be a literary work—not biography, which is bound up with literal reality ("... an existant can never justify the existence of another existant"), but a fictitious work, which would be "beautiful and hard as steel and make people ashamed of their existence":

> A book. Naturally, at first it would only be a troublesome, tiring
> work, it wouldn't stop me from existing or feeling that I exist. But a

time would come when the book would be written, when it would be
behind me, and I think that a little of its clarity might fall over my
past. Then perhaps, because of it I could remember my life without
repugnance. Perhaps one day, thinking precisely of this hour ... I
shall feel my heart beat faster and say to myself: "That was the day,
that was the hour, when it all started." And I might succeed–in the
past, nothing but the past–in accepting myself.

Placing himself in the future, with his novel already completed,
Roquentin imagines himself looking back to the present moment, when he
decided to write the book. The finished novel will represent for him a kind
of triumph over existence, or Being; with it he will presumably join the
composer and songstress of "Some of these days ... (who "washed themselves of the sin of existing"). This of course suggests bad faith. By relying
on the artistic rigor of the novel to counteract the onrush of Being, he
hopes to "accept" himself by means of the finished book, even though the
book, once completed, is no longer "his" and any attempt to possess it is
doomed to failure. However, Roquentin is well aware that the finished
book, like the record, can bring him only momentary respite from existence, from which he can never be free, even in his death. He knows that,
looking back, he will accept himself in "nothing but the past," that period
beginning now, with his conception of the book, and ending at that point
when he will have completed it. By implication, what will be the present
then will in its turn require a new enterprise, the future completion of
which will justify that present (which will have become the past), to be
followed by still another project for the new present, and so on. Roquentin's solace, then, lies not in the finished novel but in the act of writing it.
It lies, simply, in action for its own sake, the clear and deliberate retort to
the challenge of existence.

Roquentin's solution is quite modest–he does not expect much from it.
He knows that while it will enable him to escape the nausea, it will not
affect existence itself, which must forever remain senseless, amorphous and
inscrutable. At best, his new project will provide him the means of
adjusting to existence and, possibly, of accepting himself. And although
writing a novel is more compatible to him than putting together a
biography, his life will continue to be barren and austere. With his insight
into being he is even less likely to marry or form other deep attachments.
Nor will he ever admire again the example of the bourgeois embracing in

bad faith such abstractions as God, country, honor, duty and the like. The flux of existence has taught him that there are no absolutes or fixed values, no bright haven at the end of the road. In honesty and lucidity, he sees his new commitment for what it is: a tentative gesture, an action with an uncertain end, promising only fleeting comfort for the pain of living and none for the inevitability of dying.

Chapter 5

Albert Camus: *The Myth of Sisyphus,*
                 The Rebel, and
                 The Fall

Although Camus does not necessarily deny the existence of God, his portrait of the man without faith is as stark as Sartre's. Camus' extreme skepticism leads him to the question that any underground man must sooner or later ask: Is life worth living? He begins his germinal essay in *The Myth of Sisyphus and Other Essays,* "An Absurd Reasoning," with the provocative assertion that "there is but one truly serious philosophical problem, and that is suicide."[1]

THE MYTH OF SISYPHUS

People commit suicide for a variety of reasons: ill-health, loss of wealth, betrayal and disappointment in love, guilt and self-hatred. But all suicides have one element in common: despair. Inherent in despair is a contradiction: to lose hope, one must first have had it. Although Camus finally rejects despair, he retains the essential element of despair—the perpetual tension between yearning and frustration. This contradiction Camus calls the *absurd.* The concept of the absurd is hardly new in the history of thought. Neither is the extraordinary importance Camus assigns to it. What is unique is Camus' answer to the challenge of the absurd.

[1] Albert Camus, *The Myth of Sisyphus and Other Essays,* tr. Justin O'Brien, New York, 1955. Subsequent quotations from *The Myth of Sisyphus and Other Essays* are from this edition.

Camus, like his great predecessor Descartes, resolves to begin his enquiry from a position of strict empiricism, or doubt. He strips himself of all assumptions, admitting only the initial truths of his own feelings and sensations, e.g., he knows that he exists as perceiver and that there is a world around him to be perceived. From these self-evident beginnings he will draw his conclusions, taking nothing on faith and following his logic wherever it will lead him. This implies, of course, not only an open mind, but maximum consciousness; not just intellectual awareness, but optimum sensibility, alertness and receptiveness to experience as well.

What he immediately discovers is a fundamental contradiction between the world as it now presents itself to him and the conception he has always had of it. Prior to this awakening he took for granted that the universe was a coherent unity, patterned around knowable and unshakeable laws, and that man was a vital part of this whole. He now sees only a dislocated and insubstantial world, which not only eludes his attempts to explain it but which is also totally indifferent to him. Suddenly, he experiences himself as an intruder upon another planet, and a feeling of derangement and unreality takes hold of him:

> What, then, is that incalculable feeling that deprives the mind of the sleep necessary to life? A world that can be explained even with bad reasons is a familiar world. But, on the other hand, in a universe suddenly divested of illusions and lights, man feels an alien, a stranger. His exile is without remedy since he is deprived of the memory of a lost home or the hope of a promised land. This divorce between man and his life, the actor and his setting, is properly the feeling of absurdity. All healthy men having thought of their own suicide, it can be seen that there is a direct connection between this feeling and the longing for death.

The "divorce" that Camus refers to intensifies as he pushes logic to its utmost limits. In pursuit of the ultimate nature (the *whatness*) of reality and the final cause (the *why*) of our actions, reason runs up against "absurd walls," which abruptly terminate rational analysis. While he can perceive the secondary properties of things, describe and catalogue them and enumerate their effects, he cannot tell what these things are in themselves. For example, he experiences hardness, softness, roughness, smoothness, and so forth. But turning to science for a definition of matter—its essence apart from its secondary properties—he is forced to resort to a metaphor: matter is an organized system of electrons and protons, with the electrons gravitating around the protons like planets around the sun. He encounters the same difficulty when he tries to apprehend something as basic as his own identity. He can be fairly certain of the facts that constitute his "self"—his acts and feelings, his physical characteristics, his upbringing—but when he puts these data together the resultant "whole" is only a shadowy paradigm of how he actually experiences himself: the data are both more and less than the self and, in any event, add up to only an arbitrary approximation of it:

> Of whom and of what indeed can I say: "I know that!" This heart within me I can feel, and I judge that it exists. This world I can touch, and I likewise judge that it exists. There ends all my knowledge, and the rest is construction. For if I try to seize this self of which I feel sure, if I try to define and to summarize it, it is nothing but water slipping through my fingers. . . . Between the certainty I have of my existence and the content I try to give to that assurance, the gap will never be filled.

Camus challenges the value of the reasoning process itself. In his attack on logic, he quotes Aristotle's enunciation (in the *Metaphysics*) of the following paradox:

> ". . . by asserting that all is true we assert the truth of the contrary assertion and consequently the falsity of our own thesis (for the contrary assertion does not admit that it can be true). And if one says that all is false, that assertion is itself false. If we declare that solely the assertion opposed to ours is false or else that solely ours is not false, we are nevertheless forced to admit an infinite number of true or false judgments. For the one who expresses a true assertion proclaims simultaneously that it is true, and so on *ad infinitum*."

But logical paradox does not necessarily portend the breakdown of logic, nor do the limitations of scientific inquiry undermine the trustworthiness of science. Camus, as well as Aristotle, uses logic even as he is demonstrating its limitations! The modern logician would resolve the above paradox by substituting abstract symbols for the key terms, distinguishing between the formal structure ("validity") of the statement and its application ("truth") and rejecting the latter as being outside the domain of pure logic. Nor would the modern physicist be daunted by Camus' questioning of the planetary metaphor for matter. The metaphor "works," enabling us to build bridges and send rockets to the moon, and is therefore at least one kind of "knowledge." The scientist claims only to describe patterns of behavior in matter (and his descriptions, or models, are subject to modification); he does not presume to define the ultimate, irreducible nature of matter.

Camus is asking for what only the mystic has claimed to achieve, total and unconditional knowledge of reality. As a rationalist, however, the Absurd Man must reject mysticism. Yet though his demand is emotional and unreasonable, he can no more suppress it than he can stop breathing. In fact, as we shall see later, suicide and the suppression of this urge for ultimate knowledge are one and the same.

Subjecting his actions to the same rigorous scrutiny as he did reality, the Absurd Man now sees them as purposeless and mechanical. They take on a comical, nonsensical aspect. Camus asks us to imagine a man talking on a telephone whom we can see but not hear. In another essay he offers, as an analogy to modern man, ancient Sisyphus, who was doomed to regularly roll a rock up a hill only to see it roll right back down. We could cite innumerable other instances from our daily lives: a television commercial with the sound turned off or a series of commentators broadcasting the same news items all day; the elaborate preparations for a dinner that is disposed of in a few minutes; the regular punching of the time clock in order to live in order to continue punching the time clock; the frugality, the building for the future, the dreams and aspirations, the lifetime of ceaseless activity, all culminating in the crowning absurdity, which is death.[2]

Since he has rejected from the outset anything that he cannot immediately experience, the Absurd Man, like the Existentialist, must reject an afterlife. But death not only terminates life; it also negates the "meaning" of life, at least of that considerable part of our existence that we spend in pursuit of goals. An action has purpose, and therefore meaning, when it is done *for the sake* of something. A purposeful action looks beyond itself to some future result, or realization. Death precludes the future. It severs the chain of cause and effect, motive and action, by means of which we direct our lives. Unless we postulate something beyond ourselves, something that outlives and justifies our actions in spite of our death—unless we presup-

---

[2] The absurd, of course, is an essential element of each of the novels that we are considering in our study. It is also powerfully dramatized in the plays of Ionesco, Beckett, Genet and other dramatists of the Theatre of the Absurd.

pose God—then death ultimately renders our actions meaningless. But again, as a rational-empiricist, the Absurd Man must deny God. Camus, with Sartre, contends that if God exists, He is irrelevant, since we have no direct or certain knowledge of Him. What we do experience, given God's existence, is only the irrational universe, which may or may not be His creation. All that we can be certain of is the moment, not because we can know it (formulate and define it) but because we experience it, and experience nothing else. Moreover, each moment is discrete; to conceive of life as a continuum, or flow, is to make a projection into the unrealized and therefore nonexistent future. Like Sartre, Camus sees human life, not as a continuous river, but as the ice floes within the river; and living, as hopping from one floe to the next until the distant shore is reached.

So far, Camus depicts a bleak portrait of the Absurd Man. Isolated, without hope or certainty, confronting in each moment a world that is strange and often hostile to him, forced to demand what he cannot have yet remaining acutely conscious of his deprivation, the Absurd Man at this point resembles underground man.

Camus certainly knew that many people go through life hardly aware of anything absurd in human existence. It is not to these people that he addressed himself, but to the highly conscious reader, who "having become conscious of the absurd is forever bound to it." The absurd experience is not passive. Rather, it is the result of a confrontation between human consciousness and an irrational universe: the subject with his expectations ("nostalgia") and the object (the frustrating world) are "characters" in an existential encounter, or "drama," out of which springs the absurd:

> At this point of his effort man stands face to face with the irrational. He feels within him his longing for happiness and for reason. The absurd is born of this confrontation between the human need and the unreasonable silence of the world. This must not be forgotten. This must be clung to because the whole consequence of a life can depend on it. The irrational, the human nostalgia, and the absurd that is born of their encounter—these are the three characters in the drama that must necessarily end with all the logic of which an existence is capable.

One can, of course, escape this dilemma by removing either the subject (agent) or the object (world). The obliteration of the first is literal suicide.

Denial of the second is what Camus calls "philosophical suicide," or Kierkegaard's "leap of faith," by means of which one affirms that the world is rational and harmonious to some omniscient higher being even though that order is not apparent to human reason.

But Camus categorically rejects both forms of suicide. To kill one's self is simply to shirk the problem of how to live with the absurd; to have faith in an unseen unity is to pretend that the problem does not exist. In the first case, one literally cancels himself out as a human being; in the second, he negates the essential element of human experience, which is contradiction and tension. In both cases, he evades the only truth that he can be certain of, himself in opposition to a hostile universe. Finally, suicide in either form is a resignation to the cause of his anguish ("Suicide, like the leap, is acceptance at its extreme"). By resigning himself he cooperates with the irrational; whereas, since it is the Sisyphean rock at the root of human misery, he ought, like Dostoevsky's Underground Man, to shake his fist at it. "The absurd has meaning," Camus insists, "only if it is not agreed to." To the challenge of the absurd, then, he cannot offer suicide, or passive acquiescence, or religious zeal, or any of the diverse opiates—liquor, drugs, sleeping pills, tranquilizers—that humans resort to in order to dull consciousness. He advocates revolt.

Revolt, which along with the absurd makes up the core of Camus' philosophy, affirms the dignity of man. The absurd, being an absolute and given component of human existence, is inescapable. But through revolt, the Absurd Man can at least establish an attitude—an attitude of scorn—with which to deal with it; he need not be a humiliated supplicant slavishly bowing to it. He knows that he is fighting windmills (actually, a necessary condition of the absurdist ethic, at least as it is stated in "An Absurd Reasoning," is that he first relinquish all hope of changing things). But like his ancient Stoic ancestor, Epictetus, the Absurd Man dictates how he will respond to the mocking fate that he cannot escape.[3]

Revolt, then, has become an effective tool for dealing with age-old human problems. Not only does it permit the Absurd Man a measure of control over himself (if not the world), but it also enables him to live a freer, fuller life. Having renounced hope and faith, and having genuinely confronted the fact of death, he lives only for the immediate present. He is

[3] As Epaphroditus was twisting the leg of Epictetus, his slave, the latter smilingly observed that if Epaphroditus persisted, the leg would break. When the leg finally broke, Epictetus said, "I told you so." Possibly, this anecdote is apocryphal; nonetheless, Epictetus has much in common with Camus' Absurd Man.

therefore liberated from the demands and unseen menaces of the future, experiencing a "freedom with regard to common rules." He will continue to make plans for the future; but whether they materialize or collapse, he does not lose his equanimity. Along with revolt and freedom comes "passion," the third consequence of the absurd awakening. Passionate living for Camus is wringing from each moment as much as it can yield and living as many moments as one can. Putting aside for the moment the complex question of value in Camus' thought, we can see why he lays such stress on the "quantity" (as distinguished from the "quality") of experience. The realization of death makes the moment precious. The quantity of living is a function both of the literal length of our lives and the degree of consciousness that we bring to each experience: longevity provides the number of experiences, consciousness their intensity. Thus, says Camus, "The present and the succession of presents before a constantly conscious soul is the ideal of the absurd man."

THE REBEL

In *The Rebel,* published eight years after "An Absurd Reasoning," Camus pushes his affirmation of man to the point where he not only rejects underground man but, in many respects repudiates—or at least modifies—the Absurd Man. The Absurd Man has now become the Rebel. To rebel, for Camus, now means an assertion of belief in *something.* "Rebellion, though apparently negative, since it creates nothing, is profoundly positive in that it reveals the part of man which must always be defended."[4] Revolt, then, is both the measure and expression of value. But while Camus still rejects God—there is no Moses conveniently handing out commandments—he argues, like Kant and Sartre, that value can only be experienced as universal. When one says something is "right," he means it is right without qualification. Camus rejected suicide (or self-murder) because it cancelled out the absurd encounter; he now condemns all murder:

> But it is obvious that absurdism hereby admits that human life is the
> only necessary good since it is precisely life that makes the encounter

[4] Albert Camus, *The Rebel,* tr. Anthony Bower, New York, 1956. Subsequent quotations from *The Rebel* are from this edition.

possible and since, without life, the absurdist wager would have no
basis. . . . From the moment that life is recognized as good, it becomes
good for all men.

Camus has, in fact, substituted humanism for God while retaining the
ethical substance of the world's great religions. Humanity, in the purest
meaning of the term, has become Camus' absolute:

> Thus we understand that rebellion cannot exist without a strange
> form of love. Those who find no rest in God or in history are
> condemned to live for those who, like themselves, cannot live: in fact,
> for the humiliated.

The Absurd Man, having begun with the assumption that anything is
permissible, has by his revolt imposed on himself what Camus calls
"limits"—the point beyond which his actions are inimical to human life,
freedom and dignity.[5]

It is difficult to avoid the conclusion that Camus here has made his own
leap of faith. In "An Absurd Reasoning," he unequivocally rejected an
absolute scale of values (though he implies there might be subjective
values):

> Belief in the meaning of life always implies a scale of values, a choice,
> our preferences. Belief in the absurd, according to our definitions,
> teaches the contrary.

In *The Rebel,* Camus has suddenly reaffirmed the Golden Rule. Between the
writing of these two essays Camus lived through the Nazi atrocities of
World War II. Clearly the amorality of "An Absurd Reasoning" condones
these mass murders. But the humanitarianism of *The Rebel,* while it
expresses Camus' personal feelings, does not follow from his absurdist
premises, which are still the basis for his philosophy in the later book. With
his denial of an absolute basis for ethics, such as God, and with his
insistence that the world is irrational and therefore beyond our
comprehension, on what basis can Camus say it is categorically wrong to
commit murder? If the only thing that I can know for certain is that I

[5] Inevitably, the question comes up: Under what circumstances, if any, is murder justified?
For Camus' somewhat complicated answer to this question, the reader is referred to the
section in *The Rebel* entitled "Historical Murder," pp. 286-293.

cannot know, then how can I tell the difference between right and wrong? How, indeed, do I know that there is one?

Camus argues that if suicide is wrong then so is murder, because we experience value as universal. But to experience a right as if it were universal and absolute does not mean that it is in fact universal and rooted in the very nature of things. (Sartre very carefully made that distinction in his analysis of anguish and referred to his humanism as "subjective.") Only an omniscient observer, who can see beyond man, can determine the objectivity and universality of value; and, as we have seen, absurdist philosophy cannot admit that there is such an omniscience. For the same reason, Camus' choice of revolt over suicide is questionable. His justification of that course is that suicide cancels the absurd "encounter" while revolt keeps it alive. But why should the absurd be kept alive? The fact that it is an unavoidable component of human life does not necessarily mean that it is a desirable one. Indeed, it is the absurd which prompts us to contemplate suicide in the first place. Camus is saying that in order to live the best life possible, we should remain conscious of the absurd at all times; and that in order to be conscious of the absurd, we must stay alive! He describes Sisyphus' triumph[6] as he watches his rock roll down the hill, knowing that he will have to roll it up the hill again and that it will roll right back down, ad infinitum. The average man, unimpressed with this perverse "victory," would be more tempted to sit down and cry at this point.

By the time we have got through *The Rebel,* Camus' hero (formerly Absurd Man, now Rebel) bears less resemblance to underground man than he does to the romantic Resistance fighter of World War II, who in fact did provide much of the inspiration for that book. The divergence between the Rebel and underground man begins in their mode of revolt. Revolt for Camus' hero becomes an affirmation of life and a force for positive change. For underground man it must always end in helpless rage and despair. Consciousness and sensibility, at the core of the attitude of both men, enhances living for the Rebel while it only intensifies underground man's suffering. And freedom, an inescapable fact of existence for both men, takes on for them distinctive, at times antithetical, forms. Camus' initial

---

[6] "Sisyphus, proletarian of the gods, powerless and rebellious, knows the whole extent of his wretched condition: it is what he thinks of during his descent. The lucidity that was to constitute his torture at the same time crowns his victory. There is no fate that cannot be surmounted by scorn." (*The Myth of Sisyphus and Other Essays,* p. 90)

"freedom from common rules" has suddenly assumed "limits," and the Rebel thus takes his place in a human fraternity stretching from Socrates swallowing the hemlock to Winston Churchill making the victory sign at that juncture in history when Camus was having second thoughts about "An Absurd Reasoning." Underground man, whose freedom is curtailed only by physical and external necessity, is doomed to occupy a universe in which anything is possible: for him there is only the dizzying sensation of infinity and the horror of the void.

THE FALL

The absurd takes many forms in Camus' major fiction. In *The Stranger* it is society itself, primarily its legal system, which condemns a self-confessed murderer not for the murder he has committed, but for the fact that he is a nonconformist. In addition to a flawed society, Camus seems to suggest a potential infirmity in human nature: in *The Stranger* Merseult's shooting of the Arab is totally senseless, i.e., absurd, being precipitated by the concomitant causes of the merciless Algerian sun, the headiness of the wine Merseult has just drunk, and the blinding flash of the Arab's knife. In *The Plague* the absurd is unmistakably nature, both as the literal bubonic plague descending upon a helpless city and as the symbolic plague, the potential evil in man's nature, manifesting itself in war, capital punishment (legalized murder), and other instances of inhumanity.[7] Inhumanity (including mere indifference to the suffering of others) is a major theme of Camus' last novel, *The Fall*. Here, however, Camus focuses less on the misery of the victim than he does on the guilt of the offender and, by extension, the problem of human guilt in general.

In each novel, man is prey to the inexplicable and paradoxical, which is beyond his power to control. What is permitted him is the attitude that he can adopt to the absurd. The protagonists of *The Plague*–Rieux, Dr. Tarrou, Rambert, indeed a whole city–choose the position of Camus' Rebel by heroically fighting the plague. Even the apparent anti-hero of *The Stranger,* Merseult, revolts in the closing pages of the novel. His revolt, it is

---

[7] In his play *State of Siege,* on the same theme, Camus stresses the symbolic meaning of plague, viz., evil. The abstract character, The Plague, is not invincible: if men choose to, they can thwart it; however, they can never destroy it, and it perpetually lies in wait to assert itself when they relax their guard.

true, coincides with the certainty of his death; nonetheless, in his spirited scorn of his executioners he takes his place beside triumphant Sisyphus sneering at the gods. Therefore, while they are all harried by the absurd, they are not underground men. For an unequivocal example of underground man in Camus' novels, we must turn to Jean Baptiste Clamence in *The Fall*.

Unmarried, essentially friendless, unemployed and free of social commitments of any kind, Jean Baptiste Clamence is a voluntary exile in Amsterdam. He is middle-aged and in declining health, suffering from recurring bouts of malaria and, like Underground Man, from a bad liver, which is the result of excessive drinking. He lives in a shabby room, the door to which he apprehensively bolts at night, and spends most of his time in a disreputable bar nearby; his drinking companions are generally crooks, prostitutes and assorted shady characters whom he occasionally defends in the law courts, having once been a highly successful criminal lawyer. From time to time, he corners a respectably attired transient passing through his favorite bar, to whom he tells the story of his "fall."

Prior to his arrival on Amsterdam's "skid row," Clamence had led what, in the eyes of men, would be considered the truly successful life. Handsome and in excellent health, popular alike with men and women, active in a wide range of interests, a subscriber to liberal causes and humanistic societies, he was, in his personal life, enviable. He was also a glittering success in his law practice. His renown as a lawyer was owing not only to his skill in the court, but also to the "noble cases" that he specialized in: either widows, orphans and the poor, from whom he accepted no fee; or "headline" murderers whom more cautious lawyers avoided. Robin Hood of the bar, innocent himself of having either committed a crime or of punishing the criminal, he took special pride in rescuing his trembling client from the fury of the law:

> The judges punished and the defendants expiated, while I, free of any duty, shielded from judgment as from penalty, I freely held sway bathed in a light as of Eden.[8]

His fall began with another fall, that of a young woman who drowned herself in the Seine as Clamence walked by and did nothing to save her.

---

[8] Albert Camus, *The Fall*, tr. Justin O'Brien, New York, 1956. Subsequent quotations from *The Fall* are from this edition.

Though he was able to put the suicide out of his mind for several years, it eventually surfaced. One day, crossing the same bridge, he imagined he heard laughter issuing from the river. The laughter, viz., the signalling of his guilt, was Clamence's absurd awakening, from which he was never to recover. From that point on he "lost track of the light, the mornings, the holy innocence of those who forgive themselves."

Suddenly, Clamence was not the man he had thought he was. Instead of a free and generous humanitarian, he realized that he was a self-centered, uncommitted man who had lived for his own pleasure and for the figure he cut in public. He now saw that his charity had actually been a velvet whip: his defense of the underdog had been a skillful maneuver by which he simultaneously put the client under his obligation, triumphed over the judge, and avoided any identification of himself with either the judged or the judging:

> My profession satisfied most happily that vocation for summits. . . . It set me above the judge whom I judged in turn, above the defendant whom I forced to gratitude. Just weigh this, *cher monsieur*, I lived with impunity. I was concerned in no judgment; I was not on the floor of the courtroom, but somewhere in the flies like those gods that are brought down by machinery from time to time to transfigure the action and give it its meaning.

With the laughter, and a series of bizarre events that followed it, he was pulled down (or "fell") from those flies. He discovered that he too had always had an itch to judge and that he had always been judged by others. With this realization, he began to experience a gradual breakdown. First his profession fell to pieces. Then friends and lovers, his "humanism," life itself turned sour. His idealism and self-respect metamorphosed into cynicism and self-loathing. The superego in him was now raging; everywhere he heard the mocking laugh. To silence it, he resorted to underground man's usual palliatives and cauterizers: heavy drinking, sexual debauchery, wild outbursts and frenetic exertions followed by fatigue and torpor, the relentless whipping of body and mind while balking at the clean, definitive limit of suicide. As a last desperate measure Clamence quit Paris for Amsterdam and became a "judge-penitent."

His flight to Amsterdam was dictated by more than the necessity for a change of scene. Grey, damp and foggy, hemmed in by an unchanging sea and strapped by a series of concentric canals, like the circles of Hell,

Amsterdam expresses for Clamence his own limbo. Holland is a dream peopled with "Lohengrins":

> ... dreamily riding their black bicycles with high handle bars, funereal swans constantly drifting throughout the whole land, around the seas, along the canals.

Clamence feels a particular kinship with the Dutch, in whom he reads his own double nature. "I like them, for they are double. They are here and elsewhere." Beneath their solid bourgeois exterior stir ancestral vestiges, and the merchant burgher sitting before his spotless window dreams of Java and Cipango and the other remote reaches of the Dutch colonial empire, where "men die mad and happy."

On the other hand, as the epigraph to the novel clearly implies, *The Fall* is intended to depict not just Amsterdam, but Western society in general.[9] Other writers in other cities have described the stark and equivocal atmosphere that Clamence attributes to Amsterdam. It belongs to the St. Petersburg of Dostoevsky's *Notes from Underground* (with its "wet" and "dingy" and "yellow" snow) or the London of Eliot's "The Love Song of J. Alfred Prufrock" (with its "half-deserted streets," "its muttering retreats," its fog curling up like a cat). Nor is duality, or hypocrisy, unique to the Dutchman. It is not with the native of Amsterdam, but with the foreign traveler passing through the city, that Clamence plays his incredible game of judge-penitent, which presupposes that duality in men.

Clamence's guilt, which is inescapable, is also too much for him to bear; he must therefore live with it as one with a chronic ailment to which he applies continual medication. By a perverse "stroke of genius," the relief he hits upon is to "thin" it out by inflicting it on others (as a dope addict is said to "turn on" others so as to share his misery with them): "Hence I had to find another means of extending judgment to everybody in order to make it weigh less heavily on my own shoulders." But bitter experience has taught him that he cannot judge others with impunity. Therefore, he sophistically reasons, if he first punishes himself (through penitence) he

---

[9] Taken from Lermontov's *A Hero of Our Time*, the epigraph reads: "Some were dreadfully insulted, and quite seriously, to have held up as a model such an immoral character as *A Hero of Our Time*; others shrewdly noticed that the author had portrayed himself and his acquaintances.... *A Hero of Our Time*, gentlemen, is in fact a portrait, but not of an individual; it is the aggregate of the vices of our whole generation in their fullest expression."

will earn the "right" to judge others: "Inasmuch as every judge some day
ends up as a penitent, one had to travel the road in the opposite direction
and practice the profession of penitent to be able to end up as a judge." He
will thus establish a community of guilt. And his method will be that of the
skillful evangelist who, having first confessed his unworthiness, draws from
his inspired audience a kindred confession:

> Covered with ashes, tearing my hair, my face scored by clawing, but
> with piercing eyes, I stand before all humanity recapitulating my
> shames without losing sight of the effect I am producing, and saying:
> "I was the lowest of the low." Then imperceptibly I pass from the "I"
> to the "we." When I get to "This is what we are," the trick has been
> played and I can tell them off. I am like them . . . we are in the soup
> together.

With the macabre invention of the judge-penitent (more sinister than the
role-playing of any of the other underground men), Clamence has
presumably brought his guilt under control.

For the moment, we need not concern ourselves with the effectiveness of
this solution, or whether Clamence is really serious. What we should take
note of at this point is Camus' astute analysis of guilt. The self-destructive
power of guilt was a major concern of each of the writers taken up thus far.
In addition, Camus, like Dostoevsky, sees in guilt a potential force for evil
in general. Ostensibly, Clamence pronounces judgment on himself for
having failed to save the girl. Actually, that judgment is merely the
conscious formulation of a deeper, more subtle and pervasive sense of his
unworthiness, which Clamence is hardly aware of. But whatever its origins,
Clamence's self-hatred, contrary to Kafka's, becomes indiscriminate hatred;
and just as love of his own life led to love of all life for Camus' Rebel, so
self-disgust for guilt-ridden Clamence leads to loathing for all men. When
he hears the "confessions" of his interlocutors, he is only corroborating his
initial conviction that men are depraved.

Clamence, like Kafka and his protagonists, now sees the world as one
vast courtroom in which each of us plays his role as judge or defendant.
Guilt and punishment constitute a universal vicious circle: all men are
guilty, they are punished for their guilt, they punish for having been
punished, they feel guilt for having punished, and so on and so forth.
Hence, for Clamence, the worst scoundrel is the severest judge. Moreover,
since the judge has power over the condemned man, we are all alternately

masters and slaves (men no longer need God the Prime Master; they have one another). The most humble and lowly person has at least one victim to tyrannize over, if only his dog.[10] Only the rare soul escapes this cycle and is thus free. But freedom to us is repugnant; for in breaking through this universal pattern, we banish ourselves from the community of men, who have set it up as their law. For Clamence, as for every other underground protagonist, freedom is a "chore":

> I didn't know that freedom is not a reward or a decoration that is celebrated with champagne. Nor yet a gift, a box of dainties designed to make you lick your chops. Oh, no! It's a chore, on the contrary, and a long-distance race, quite solitary and very exhausting. No champagne, no friends raising their glasses as they look at you affectionately. Alone in a forbidding room, alone in the prisoner's box before the judges, and alone to decide in face of oneself or in the face of others' judgment. At the end of all freedom is a court sentence; that's why freedom is too heavy to bear, especially when you're down with a fever, or are distressed, or love nobody.

Doubtless, Clamence's obsession with human guilt, and his conviction that men are consequently cruel, results in part from his deranged state of mind. He is not entirely normal after the suicide; he even has touches of paranoia, imagining that people are laughing at him. Nonetheless, however exaggerated his observations may be, they, like the imprecations of Roquentin and Underground Man before him, ring too true to be dismissed as the ravings of a madman. Clamence's examples from history and the world around him suggest, even, that he has done some research on the subject. Camus, of course, does not share his hero-narrator's unqualified low opinion of people. In *The Plague,* for example, Camus portrays a whole city acting heroically. Yet he would agree with the substance, if not the intensity, of Clamence's criticism: there is guilt in the world, and it is the cause of needless suffering.

Clamence's distinction between the pagan and the Judaic-Christian attitudes toward guilt is already foreshadowed in *The Rebel,* in which Camus traces guilt in Western society to that point in history when Christianity rejected its Mediterranean for its Hebraic origins. The Medi-

---

[10] For old Salamano, in Camus' *The Stranger,* beating his dog was as necessary as breathing was. When the dog finally ran off, Salamano, now deprived of his victim, was heartbroken.

terranean, or Hellenic, emphasis on nature and freedom gave way to the
Hebraic passion for organization and the Law.[11] This shift resulted in the
superbly structured, autocratic Church, with its complex theology built
around the doctrine of sin (the Fall) and its extraordinary system of rewards
and punishments. Clamence may very well be speaking for Camus, then,
when he assigns to Christ himself a sense of guilt. Christ—not the Son of
God, but a man who grew up in Judaic society—was "guilty" of the
Slaughter of the Innocents. Numbers of children were slain because Herod
had been forewarned that one of them would become the Messiah.
Paradoxically, Christ did not will their deaths yet they died because of him.
He was guilty of an "innocent crime," which he himself acknowledged:
"Knowing what he knew . . . he found it too hard for him to hold on and
continue." Thus even Christ, whose mission was presumably to wash away
guilt, could not escape it. And we are reminded of Steppenwolf's
melancholy conclusion, "One's born and at once one is guilty."

Camus, therefore, disputes neither the prevalence of guilt nor its potentiality for evil. What he finds objectionable is Clamence's "definitive
solution" to the problem (the allusion to the Nazi extermination camps is
deliberate). It is, in fact, the Clamences of the world who, wallowing in
their own guilt, would torment other guilty souls. Guilt may be inevitable
but judgment is not. This conclusion can easily be inferred from *The Rebel*,
with its advocacy of love and humanitarianism. But it is explicit in *The Fall*
as well. Even Clamence, in those instants when his lucidity breaks through
the grinning mask of his cynicism, can admit of at least one man whose
guilt did not drive him to judge others. Ironically, it is the very man in
whose name people do judge, Jesus Christ.

---

[11] This distinction for Camus between nature and history is a tool for analyzing the whole
of history and is at the core of the argument of *The Rebel*. Briefly, it expresses the conflict
between natural man and historical regimes. In the first view, the individual has natural, or
inalienable, rights; he is an end in himself provided he observe limits, i.e., respect the same
rights in others. It is, in fact, the position of the Rebel outlined above. In the second view,
whatever rights an individual has are conferred on him by a preestablished social system or
order, which can at its discretion deprive him of them; moreover, he himself is dispensable,
existing first and foremost as a means to the realization of the purposes of that system. This
is the position not only of the Church in the Middle Ages but of any absolutist,
"historically necessary" system, such as Fascism and Communism. Thus in *The Plague*,
Father Paneloux goes unchallenged when he argues that the Christian must either accept
God totally, and with Him the plague, or reject Him totally. The Communist must
likewise accept the Stalinist massacres as necessary or renounce Communism. (This is, of
course, the point made by Arthur Koestler, who collaborated with Camus on *Reflections on
Capital Punishment*.)

"Who will cast the first stone?" Christ asked. His tolerance and mercy represent a sharp break with the Hebraic god of wrath, at the same time that Christ was under sentence for breaking one of that god's commandments. He knew that all men were guilty but that our human obligation was to alleviate, not add to, the burden of that guilt. So instead of implicating others in his guilt, he bore the brunt of it alone. Indeed, as we have seen, his guilt was his "cross," which he literally carried to his death! With this stoic resignation, this icy loneliness in the last hour, this willingness to atone, Christ broke the vicious circle of guilt and punishment. He was therefore a free man.

But Christ, for Camus, was only a man, who made his peace only with men. He still had a score to settle with his god. Although in the eyes of men he had accepted responsibility for the Slaughter of the Innocents, he had hoped that another judgment, prior to and superseding human wisdom, would vindicate, would uphold him.[12] But the skies over Calvary, like Kafka's Castle, were mute, neither absolving him nor explicating the mystery of his guilt, that is, the absurd:

> He was not upheld, he complained, and as a last straw, he was censored. Yes, it was the third evangelist, I believe, who first suppressed his complaint. "Why hast thou forsaken me?"—it was a seditious cry, wasn't it?

This, and not the crucifixion per se, was the real tragedy of Christ according to the retelling of his story in *The Fall* (whether we attribute it to Clamence alone or both Clamence and Camus). Christ died "guilty" of murder yet was not a murderer: he never received the ultimate voucher of his innocence even though "Thou shalt not kill" could not literally be applied to him. Paradoxically, having rebelled against the whole system of judgment that had first condemned him, he died awaiting exoneration by that system. Christ, in Clamence's version of the Christian myth, suffered a hell that few "sinners" are capable of imagining—he was punished believing at the same time that he should not be punished:

---

[12] Camus here conceives of freedom as Sartre does: it is a burden and a responsibility, and the attempt to deny it (and its consequences) is "bad faith." We must not, of course, push the similarities here between Sartre and Camus too far. Sartre would never consider Christ guilty in the first place. For Sartre, one is responsible only for what he voluntarily chooses; he properly "despairs" of—disclaims responsibility for—something that somebody else does without consulting him, even though it is done in his name. In the final analysis, we cannot even be certain that Camus really attributed to Christ responsibility for the Slaughter of the Innocents, inasmuch as the speaker is actually Clamence.

> He who clings to a law does not fear the judgment that reinstates him
> in an order that he believes in. But the keenest of human tortures is to
> be judged without a law.

Christ was ultimately thwarted by an ambiguous world order (the absurd).
Yet in his uncompromising insistence on vindication from his god, on the
one hand, and in his refusal to inflict misery on his fellowman on the other,
he embodies for Camus the highest expression of the absurd tragic hero and
the Rebel. To the very end he combined in himself the freedom of Sartre's
anguished Existentialist, the stoic scorn of absurdist Sisyphus, and the
humanity and grace of the Rebel interceding between man and the absurd.

In his personal realization of guilt, and in his discovery of the almost
universal cruelty that results from guilt, Clamence's experience parallels
Christ's. But here the similarity stops. Instead of revolting against a scheme
of things based on guilt and judgment, Clamence actually perpetuates it.
His revolt, then, is another sham. Presumably he renounced his old way of
life in Paris; yet at the end of the novel he is happily (so he tells us) doing
all the things he had done before his fall: living for himself and his pleasures
and, above all, judging others:

> No excuses ever, for anyone; that's my principle at the outset. I
> deny the good intention, the respectable mistake, the indiscretion, the
> extenuating circumstance. With me there is no giving of absolution
> or blessing. Everything is simply totted up, and then: "It comes to so
> much. You are an evil-doer, a satyr, a congenital liar, a homosexual,
> an artist, etc." Just like that. Just as flatly. In philosophy as in politics,
> I am for the theory that refuses to grant man innocence and for any
> practice that treats him as guilty. You see in me, *très cher,* an
> enlightened advocate of slavery.

Though he is a "penitent" judge now, he is a judge nonetheless. Moreover,
even his penance is suspect. If he is doing penance for past cruelties, then
repetition of those cruelties in the role of the punishing judge contradicts
that repentance. He assures us that the only real difference between him and
other men, including his earlier self, is that he is now more conscious of his
guilt. Indeed, he actually wallows in his guilt, deriving a masochistic
pleasure from his "charming repentance." But he extracts a reward for this
elaborate self-flagellation – the "right" to condemn other sufferers.

Contrary to the true Rebel, who actively opposes the absurd, Clamence
has curiously made his own "leap of faith." He has chosen the absurd as his

gospel. It may be false: it eludes human understanding and is the source of worldly suffering. Yet, and perhaps for this very reason, he affirms it and serves it with the passion and dedication of the saint. Judge-penance is the new religion and Jean Baptiste its prophet. Just as his "revolt" and "penance" parody the example of Christ, so his name, Jean Baptiste Clamence, deliberately parodies Christ's harbinger, John the Baptist. John the Baptist prepared the populace for the new messiah, who would forgive them their sins and lead them to eternal life. Jean Baptiste Clamence, i.e., *John the Baptist of Clemency,* announces his truth—the gospel of perpetual guilt and damnation. Clamence, then, is the false prophet in the wilderness:

> ... having taken refuge in a desert of stones, fogs, and stagnant waters—an empty prophet for shabby times, Elijah without a messiah, choked with fever and alcohol, my back up against this moldy door, my finger raised toward a threatening sky, showering imprecations on lawless men who cannot endure my judgment.

Although Clamence narrates his own story in *The Fall,* we have been able to mark the point where Camus disengages himself from his erratic narrator-hero. What we also suspect, however, is that Clamence himself does not take every word of his narrative literally. He must certainly see through the preposterousness of his role as judge-penitent. Who better than he must know that it simply does not work? ("At long intervals, on a really beautiful night I occasionally hear a distant laugh and again I doubt.") Nor can we really believe that he is indifferent to the cruelty he inflicts on people by stirring up their guilt. At heart he is a sensitive, humane man who genuinely loves Christ. Who but an extreme idealist could so punish himself because he failed to risk his life for a stranger? Indeed, it is even doubtful that he could have saved the drowning woman. By the time he heard her "cries" (not her cries for help as such), the current was already carrying her away. He certainly was not heroic; but Camus (or Clamence) may be suggesting that he, Clamence, did no more nor less than most men would have done in the same circumstances, thus justifying the epigraph from Lermontov.

Therefore, whatever Clamence's relationship to Camus, on the one hand, and to the reader on the other hand, we must disentangle Clamence from the literal implications of his actions and words. What is actually dramatized in the novel is the "penitent" aspect of the judge-penitent. Since Clamence's interlocutor does not actually confess to anything, we never witness Clamence in his role as "judge": we can only reconstruct that role from the bits and pieces provided by Clamence-the-narrator, who stands between us and Clamence-the-judge. But if we cannot know what punishment he inflicts on the people who confess to him, we know what he does to himself—we see and hear him flagellating himself. *The Fall,* ultimately, is a dramatization of Clamence's self-inflicted suffering. It is, in effect, a confession, on the order of Dostoevsky's *Notes from Underground.*

The speaker, like Underground Man and some of Robert Browning's monologuists, is a tormented soul buffeted about by unresolved conflicts, which he may or may not be conscious of. He is therefore extremely complex, juggling diverse and frequently opposing masks. What he says, and even what he does, are not necessary indices of what he is. This ambiguity is reflected in his overt delivery, which is ironic, indirect and paradoxical.[13] The reader, then, must be attuned to the several voices in Clamence in order to distinguish between the polished *persona* that he presents his audience and the passion that lies behind it—a passion which he is not always aware of. Consider, for example, these extraordinary closing lines of his narrative:

> But of course you are not a policeman; that would be too easy. What? Ah, I suspected as much, you see. That strange affection I felt for you had sense to it then. In Paris you practice the noble profession of lawyer! I sensed that we were of the same species. Are we not all alike, constantly talking and to no one, forever up against the same questions although we know the answers in advance? Then please tell me what happened to you one night on the quays of the Seine and how you managed never to risk your life. You yourself utter the words that for years have never ceased echoing through my nights and that I shall at last say through your mouth: "O young woman, throw yourself into the water again so that I may a second time have the chance of saving both of us!" A second time, eh, what a risky suggestion! Just suppose, *cher maître,* that we should be taken literally? We'd have to go through with it. Brr . . . ! The water's so cold! But let's not worry! It's too late now. It will always be too late. Fortunately!

The first few lines are characteristic of Clamence's social manner—suave,

---

[13]Active in the theatre as producer, actor and playwright, Camus would understandably have an interest in the spoken word. In fact *The Fall,* which is a dramatic monologue, enabled him to combine his theatrical talents with his skill as a novelist.

ironical and faintly mocking. But beginning with the question, "Are we not all alike . . . ?," the tone begins to shift. Hardly perceptible at first, a note of seriousness, of passion and urgency, of near despair, breaks through the controlled elegance. It rises in a crescendo and reaches its climax with the conclusion of the quotation, ". . . saving both of us!" Then immediately, as if he were embarrassed by his outbreak, Clamence returns to his initial ironic urbanity, beginning with "A second time, eh. . . ." But these last lines (a series of short, jabbing sentences) are even harsher than the opening lines, despite their intended smoothness. They are taut and highly charged, as if Clamence were exaggerating his polished courtroom style to suppress his powerful emotions. The scorn is not entirely convincing—the idealist beneath the cynic will not remain buried. Nor are we convinced by the finality of the closing "Fortunately!" For we know that the record will be played again for the next witness who passes through town, and for the one after him, over and over again, until drink or fever finally brings the torment of this underground man to an end.

Chapter 6

Jean Genet: *Our Lady of the Flowers*

Sartre and Camus are philosophical nihilists who nonetheless seek a basis for value. Empirical in approach, they appeal to no authority beyond themselves. In Roquentin and Jean Baptiste, as in Underground Man, subjectivity becomes a crippling self-preoccupation that cuts them off not only from God but from their fellowman as well. But all three are only fictional characters in whom Sartre, Camus and Dostoevsky, respectively, sublimated whatever was underground in themselves. Even Kafka, who never transcends the underground condition of his protagonists, cannot be literally identified with them. In Genet's novels, however, Genet himself appears as underground man.

An orphan, a ward of the *Assistance Publique,* Genet was never to know any more about his parents than his mother's name and where she bore him. The consequences that followed from that ignominious birth should not surprise anyone familiar with orphans: adoption by strangers; the reformatory, the first in a succession of jails; a brief sojourn in the army (for Genet, the French Foreign Legion); years of vagabondage, of begging and privation, of petty larceny and male prostitution in the underworlds of Europe; then gradual involvement in grander forms of larceny, such as smuggling and burglary, culminating in a life sentence in prison. But unlike his brothers in the orphanages, ghettos and prisons, Genet was a poet. Through writing about his life he was discovered by the leading writers and intellectuals of France, on whose behalf that sentence was commuted, and he has not returned to prison since.

In the reformatory at Mettray, at the age of sixteen, Genet was branded an outlaw. At first he was shocked by the appellation, but then resolved to live up to it. In other words, the image, instead of characterizing the "real"

Genet (as yet unborn), became the finished portrait that the human model had to live up to. A universe had suddenly been defined for him, consisting of the "good" and the "bad," and on discovering that he had crossed the line separating them, he willed himself an outlaw:

> In order to weather my desolation when I withdrew more deeply into myself, I worked out, without meaning to, a rigorous discipline. The mechanism was somewhat as follows (I have used it since): to every charge brought against me, unjust though it be, from the bottom of my heart I shall answer yes. Hardly had I uttered the word—or the phrase signifying it—than I felt within me the need to become what I had been accused of being. I was sixteen years old. The reader has understood: I kept no place in my heart where the feeling of my innocence might take shelter. I owned to being the coward, traitor, thief and fairy they saw in me.[1]

Thereafter, with "rigorous discipline," he forced himself to think the thoughts, perform the acts, and feel the sensations of the thief and homosexual.

His initial activities in the underworld were modest (petty thievery, prostitution) and his stays in prison short. Gradually, his crimes became more serious, including armed robbery and burglary ("crashing"), and his prison sentences longer. Paralleling this development was the change in his sexual practices. At first, he was strictly the faggot, that is, the feminine partner in the homosexual act, usually under the domination and protection of older, tougher men (the "elder brother" in the reformatory). In time, as he himself became more self-assured, he assumed the masculine role more frequently (depending on how "virile" he was relative to his partner).

Repeatedly throughout his writings, Genet expresses contempt for his early attempts at crime; he also condemned himself for his faggotry. In effect, his novitiate as a criminal and his passivity as a sexual partner went hand in hand: they were expressions of his softness, timidity and vagueness of contour. The ideal hood, as he saw him, was ideally masculine—hard, sharp and powerful. (Harcamone, the heroic killer in the *Miracle of the Rose,* is characterized as an absolute "Prick.") What Genet eventually discovered was that crime and faggotry (not necessarily homosexuality) were irreconcilable, and his life might be described as the attempt to move from the squishiness of the female-faggot to the rigor of the male-hood.

[1] Jean Genet, *The Thief's Journal,* tr. Bernard Frechtman, New York, 1964, pp. 157-158.

To what extent he achieved this condition is uncertain, since he is inconsistent in the appraisals he makes of himself. Certainly his later exploits and attitudes would testify to a rugged manliness by any standard. His ferocity as a fighter, his fearlessness on dangerous jobs, his dominance over lovers, his pride, his sheer endurance—all set him off from the "little wretch who knew only hunger, physical humiliation, poverty, fear, and degradation" (*The Thief's Journal,* p. 98) and who, upon first entering prison, became the sex object of the first tough to claim him and to offer to fight for him. Genet dates his metamorphosis into a "male" with his first job as a burglar:

> During those years of softness when my personality took all sorts of forms, any male could squeeze my side with his walls, could contain me. My moral substance (and my white skin, weak bones, slack muscles, my slow gestures and their uncertainty) was without sharpness, without contour.... I wanted to be myself, and I was myself when I became a crasher. All burglars will understand the dignity with which I was arrayed when I held my jimmy, my "pen." From its weight, material, and shape, and from its function too, emanated an authority that made me a man. I had always needed that steel penis in order to free myself from my faggotry, from my humble attitudes, and to attain the clear simplicity of manliness.[2]

Clearly, Genet rejects here any identification of himself with the faggot, demonstrating that his original vow to be a faggot was not natural. Yet, in his own mind, he still fell considerably short of the ideal hood, that totally free agent who did not suffer from self-consciousness. The bold killers were heroic, whereas the ultimate motivation for Genet's criminal activities, including crashing, was always self-contempt:

> Murder is not the most effective means of reaching the subterranean world of abjection. Quite the contrary.... Other crimes are more degrading: theft, begging, treason, breach of trust, etc.; these are the ones I choose to commit, though I was always haunted by a murder which would cut me off irremediably from your world. (*The Thief's Journal,* p. 94)

Thief and faggot, then, were only roles Genet played in order to deal, however perversely, with his misfortune. Eventually, he discovered that it

[2] Jean Genet, *Miracle of the Rose,* tr. Bernard Frechtman, New York, 1966, p. 27.

was not faggot or hood per se that fascinated him, but their state of mind and being—their suffering, their isolation, their pride, and their almost inhuman freedom. Genet had sought to realize the pure essence of the outcast, or more precisely the "saint," pruned of all impurities:

> Starting from the elementary principles of morality and religion, the saint arrives at his goal if he sheds them. Like beauty—and poetry, with which I merge it—saintliness is individual. Its expression is original. However, it seems to me that its sole basis is renunciation. I therefore also associate it with freedom. But I wish to be a saint chiefly because the word indicates the loftiest human attitude, and I shall do everything to succeed. I shall use my pride and sacrifice it therein.
> (*The Thief's Journal,* pp. 187-188)

But if, as Genet claims, he did attain saintliness (*The Thief's Journal,* p. 185), it was not as a criminal or a faggot. He could imagine the perfect criminal and the perfect faggot, but like Sartre's Existentialist, he learned that he could never literally *be* them.[3] Inevitably, he saw that the purity he had been seeking was to be found only in poetry. Accordingly, he relinquished the jimmy for the pen.

As a poet, snugly tucked away in his mousy cell in Santé Prison, he could work unhampered at discovering, creating, recreating—endlessly experimenting with—the phenomena that he calls "Jean Genet." Not only did his past begin to take on a certain meaning that till then had eluded him, but the process itself—i.e., working with the heretofore chaotic, Steppenwolfian chess pieces of his life—helped to solidify him, to give him shape and possibly identity. And at this he seems to have been much more successful than Underground Man with his "notes":

> When, in the Santé Prison, I began to write, it was never because I wanted to relive my emotions or to communicate them, but rather because I hoped, by expressing them in a form that they themselves

[3] This is one of the major themes of *The Balcony.* In that drama, the men who *play* at being bishop, judge and general in the brothel (Irma's "house of illusions") are understandably terrified when they are called upon to actually *be* those august personages in the world outside. As the "Bishop" points out, reality spoils the act: "So long as we were in a room in a brothel, we belonged to our own fantasies. But once, having exposed them, having named them, having proclaimed them, we're now tied up with human beings, tied to you, and forced to go on with this adventure according to the laws of visibility." (Jean Genet, *The Balcony,* rev. ed., tr. Bernard Frechtman, New York, 1966, p. 79.)

imposed, to construct an order (a moral order) that was unknown (above all to me too). (*The Thief's Journal*, p. 154)

Like most of the protagonists who have appeared thus far throughout these pages, he found in writing a means of coping with what had happened to him. Writing enabled him to act, instead of being acted upon. Throughout his life Genet seems to have been obsessed with the problem of will. Torn between his own aggressiveness and passivity, he was fascinated by such dichotomies as masculine/feminine, art (i.e., will)/nature, son/orphan, free man/prisoner. The male initiates action (e.g., he ejaculates), the female responds (she receives his ejaculation); the free man comes and goes, the prisoner is confined; the son takes from the parent what is "rightfully" his, the foundling can only receive it as a gift; the male-artist projects his image on nature, female-nature is modified by it (he distorts nature by creating fantasies, he denies his natural sex by willing himself a faggot). It was through writing that Genet finally resolved these conflicts and converted the miseries of a lifetime into his greatest asset, an astounding will:

> This journal is not a mere literary diversion. The further I progress, reducing to order what my past life suggests, and the more I persist in the rigor of composition—of the chapters, of the sentences, of the book itself—the more do I feel myself hardening in my will to utilize, for virtuous ends, my former hardships. I feel their power. (*The Thief's Journal*, p. 52)

As a writer, Genet continued to think as an outcast, except that now, instead of acting out that role in the real world, he glorified it in poetry. Resolving to "rehabilitate persons, objects and feelings reputedly vile" (*The Thief's Journal*, p. 96), he proceeded to sanctify society's effluvia. In *Our Lady of the Flowers*, for example, he canonized a faggot and compared a killer on the gallows with Christ the Savior; called dregs of the underworld by such names as Divine, Our Lady of the Flowers, Archangel Gabriel, and First Communion; and used metaphors that outrageously combined the beautiful with the sordid, the sacred with the profane:

> "But," she said to the priest, "I'm not dead yet. I've heard the angels farting on the ceiling."[4]

---

[4] Jean Genet, *Our Lady of the Flowers*, tr. Bernard Frechtman, New York, 1963, p. 312.

Unlike traditional satirists, however, Genet does not make a frontal attack on his reader. He damns us indirectly, extolling what he calls our "underside"—in the form of pimp, faggot and bruiser. He slyly hints that we, like Baudelaire's famous "reader," are also fascinated by evil; he insinuates that we too are potential homosexuals and criminals who feel a sexual attraction for the killer and envy his crime.[5] Moreover, by making the underworld appear beautiful, he seductively invites us to assign a higher value to the dark side of our nature. Or if we absolutely refuse to identify with the less savory elements in Genet, he projects to us other facets of ourselves that we would rather keep hidden, from ourselves no less than from the world. We all suffer from a sense of impotence and finiteness. We all feel the inevitable gap between aspiration and realization. And we are all mythmakers, whose survival depends on a succession of artfully constructed roles. Genet is painful to read because he plays on our doubts and our guilt. The *exotica* of his writings become only too familiar on second reading.

By exposing the flaws in society's own image of itself, Genet appears to have turned the tables on an old antagonist. Yet it is difficult to take this inversion of the Christian ethic quite literally. Even Genet admits to a certain bravado in lavishing praises on outlaws, and that "naming them with words that usually designate what is noble was perhaps childish and somewhat facile." (*The Thief's Journal,* p. 96) Genet's whole treatment of morality is confusing. He seems to be saying that "good" is simply an established order, while "evil" is its opposite, i.e., what threatens to destroy it. He refused to commit crimes in Nazi Germany, for example, because, "It's a race of thieves. . . . If I steal here . . . I obey the customary order; I do not destroy it. I am not committing evil." (*The Thief's Journal,* p. 109) The "evil" man, then, is a rebel. But what happens if the rebel achieves his end, or if he breaks down the distinction between him and his opposite, as in fact Genet seems to have done to a substantial degree. Is he no longer "evil"? In other words, good and evil, in this sense, are relative terms that depend on one another, a dependency presumably beginning when Genet assumed the role of thief because he had been called one. The boy Genet did not have a

---

[5] In all of his major works, Genet manages, one way or another, to link his reader with sordid characters or events. In the directions to *The Blacks,* for example, he stipulates that there must be at least one white person in the audience watching the blacks act out their ritualistic revenge on white society. In *The Balcony,* Irma, mistress of the house of illusions, instructs the audience at the end of the play to go home to their own illusions and lies.

positive, instinctive sense of self. He could not say, "I am such-and-such." Rather, he had to begin with, "I am *not* such-and-such (e.g., an honest man); *therefore,* I am its opposite (a thief)." With this poetic fiction, Genet went on to create its opposite, the law-abiding citizen, who can think of himself as "good" only by evoking the image of his opposite, the lawbreaker. Thus Genet's advocate of law and order reinforces his shaky identity by condemning the Thief, while the poet-thief sublimates his initial ostracization by transforming the Thief into an icon. Like Dostoevsky's protagonist, Genet is ultimately a "retort" man. That he feels self-contempt when he compares himself with heroic hoods aggravates, but does not resolve, his dilemma. Despite his "choice" to become a criminal, Genet does not relish going to prison, let alone ending up on the gallows. As he awaits his trial in *Our Lady of the Flowers,* he is a fox before the grapes. Anticipating a prison sentence, he begins to will the prisoner's life, as he did the vocation of thief once he had been branded one. Already his imagination is converting the prison, particularly his cell, into a snug retreat cut off from the hectic world, where he can concoct fantasies and masturbate in peace. Yet he would like to be acquitted. His real fear of prison penetrates beneath any of his roles. This terror, at night, becomes an extended nightmare in which he repeatedly sees himself falling down precipices or sailing phantom ships into the void. In spite of his intricate rationalizations, he knows that prison is the realm of the dead:

> Let me therefore live between these walls for a man's lifetime. Who will be judged tomorrow? Some stranger bearing a name that was once my name. I can continue to die, until my death, amidst all these widowers. Lamp, washbasin, regulations, broom. And the straw mattress, my spouse.[6]

Genet, then, believes in the criminal and does not believe. But there is very little difference between an ambivalent code and no code at all. Value is an expression of total assent, that is, unqualified conviction translated into action, with conviction and action being necessary and coordinate terms. In Genet's case, there is conviction without action, or action without conviction, i.e., he idealizes the murderer yet does not kill or he commits petty crimes yet has contempt for them. If we assume with Sartre

[6]This and subsequent quotations are from Jean Genet, *Our Lady of the Flowers,* tr. Bernard Frechtman, New York, 1963.

that all action is proof of conviction, then Genet's moral code was that of
the criminal—to the degree that he carried it out. But if we view value as an
absolute, unconditional expression of self, then Genet was only a surrogate
hood, a game player like his literary cousins Underground Man, Jean
Baptiste Clamence, K., Roquentin and Steppenwolf.

In short, Genet's temple of evil is a fake. Although he vowed to destroy
the "customary order," he was no Lucifer-Hoodlum for whom the Principle of Negation was an absolute commitment. It is ontologically impossible for mere humans to serve absolute nothingness. An action exists;
therefore it is "something," and the "nothingness" it results in is
"nothing" only in respect to the "something" that the action destroys (as
Sartre's Nothingness depends upon Being). A philosophy of absolute
nihilism is inconsistent with life; and despite Genet's assertion that death is
the "only reality that satisfies us wholly," he rejected murder and suicide.

Ultimate value for Genet resides not in the hoodlum, but in himself. His
universe is as absurd as Camus'; and though he allows a place for God in it,
he is as indifferent as Sartre to God's presence or absence. But what survives
in Genet, as in Sartre and Camus, is personal revolt, glorified in art. Genet
is a perfect illustration both of Sartre's Existentialist and Camus' Absurd
Man. He began with "himself" as outcast but transformed that being into
a poet, who in turn flouted the outcast in society's face (Underground Man
could only stick out his tongue). Genet in his writings depicts human life
as a farce, in which we are assigned or assign ourselves empty roles, one as
arbitrary as the other, played out against the one true reality, the void. But
this is only the content of his writings. The vitality and passion with which
he tells his story is not nihilistic—his very act of writing, like Roquentin's,
is a cry for life. In other words, our concern should be more with the
personal function and subjective meaning of Genet's poetry than with the
objective commentary it makes on man. Indeed, that commentary may very
well be a lie:

> Truth is not my strong point. But "one must lie in order to be true."
> And even go beyond. What truth do I want to talk about? If it is
> really true that I am a prisoner who plays (who plays for himself)
> scenes of the inner life, you will require nothing other than a game.

*   *   *

Essentially fictionalized autobiography, *Our Lady of the Flowers* moves
between the extremes of literal fact and imaginative flights of pure lyrical
poetry. As in *Notes from Underground, Steppenwolf, Nausea* and *The Fall*, the

central character of the book is also the narrator. But the narrator, Jean Genet, tells the story not only of the character Jean, but also of several other characters whom the character Jean imagines. That is to say, two narratives weave in and out of the novel, crisscrossing and accompanying one another like two counterpointed melodies in a symphony. One is the account of Jean Genet in prison, awaiting his trial; the other is the story of a tragic homosexual queen (Divine), along with her lovers—a handsome scoundrel of a pimp (Darling Daintyfoot) and a pretty-faced killer (Our Lady of the Flowers)—and a host of other minor characters, all of whom are fantasies created by Jean as he lies in his cell, usually at night, masturbating.

His imagined characters, however, are "expressions" of Jean, functioning like Pablo and Hermine in *Steppenwolf*; through these characters Jean, like the Steppenwolf, is able to play "scenes of the inner life." In fact, the principal figure among the fantasy characters, Divine, is in all essentials Genet himself, who says ". . . in the final analysis, it is my own destiny, be it true or false, that I am draping (at times a rag, at times a court robe) on Divine's shoulders." Not only do the "facts" of Divine's life parallel those of the real Jean Genet's life, but Genet frequently merges with Divine, shifting without warning from the "she" to the "I." The other imagined characters are to Jean what they are to Divine: Jean "cherishes" Darling, for example, because he is Divine's lover, i.e., Darling becomes Jean's lover, in whose imaginary arms Jean-as-Divine lies each night masturbating. Thus Jean Genet-the-writer is watching Jean Genet-the-character having fantasies about himself in the form of Divine.

On paper these fantasies become the "saga" of Divine, from his boyhood in the country as Lou Culafroy, to his triumphant reign in the streets of Paris as the homosexual queen Divine, to his ultimate death and "sainthood." Genet's invocatory muses, to whom he also dedicates his book, are famous hoodlums and thugs, whose pictures line the walls of his cell. It is before these photographs that he conducts his nightly masturbatory rites; and since these thugs serve as models for Divine's lovers, it is ultimately with them that Genet plays his own vicarious love games.

The reader is struck by the stark solitude of Lou's childhood. A pale, shy and delicate boy whose natural feminism is reinforced by the patterns of dress that his mother imposes on him, he is shunned by the other children in the village. They immediately recognize him as someone apart—the strange boy living in the elegant slate house on the hill with the awesome, and possibly crazy, mother.

Though not literally an orphan like Genet, who never knew his parents, the fatherless Lou is, in effect, also motherless. The mother, Ernestine, while providing Lou with the basic material necessities, lives in a private phantasy world from which Lou is excluded. Her son is of interest to her only when he provides her with occasions for a gesture as, for example, when he is lying on his deathbed and Ernestine imagines him dying in a distant exotic city, like Venice, so that she can make pilgrimages to his grave. Like Genet and the other characters in the novel, particularly Divine, Ernestine is a marvelous dreamer. The slightest signal can send her flying off into the world of historical novels, pulp romances and penny dreadfuls. During these flights—and we scarcely see her anywhere else—it is dangerous for little boys to disturb her with questions or pathetic appeals for maternal comfort. Ernestine is a sham mother; "mother" is just another role, which she turns on and off at will, according to the mysterious workings of her own inner world. For Lou, she is as remote and unsubstantial as Gabrielle Genet, Genet's own phantom mother.

Lou's isolation from people gradually extends to disbelief in what they say and do, then to alienation from objects and things, until the visible world itself takes on that strangeness and absurdity that dogged Camus and the early Sartre. At too early an age, Lou experiences metaphysical emptiness (doubtless a reason why Sartre was so fascinated with Genet): for Lou, beneath the colors, lines and textures of objects and phenomena, there is only the void. Objects lose their solidity; actions, their meanings; and values—God, family, honor and especially truth—their credibility. Perhaps his most traumatic disillusionment is the discovery that "God is dead." Tampering with the tabernacle in the deserted church one day, he accidentally overturns the ciborium containing the Host. As it falls to the floor, the terrified little culprit—still a believing Catholic—expects that God and His angels will surely come thundering down upon him. But nothing happens: "And the miracle occurred. There was no miracle. God had been debunked. God was hollow. Just as a hole with any old thing around it."

The slate house he lives in is his sanctuary from the harshness of the village; within the house, his room is his retreat from the unpredictable outbursts of the mother. (For Genet, who also lived in a slate house as a child, it was the outhouse to which he escaped.) Here Lou creates his own world, fills it with imaginary figures, as Genet peoples his cubicle of a cell with phantasy lovers. Like Underground Man, Lou turns in upon himself: "real" life becomes a poem, or a play, with Lou as protagonist and the room as stage. In his room he accomplishes what he is unable to do outside. For example, when for some inexplicable reason Ernestine tells him he may not take violin lessons, he cuts a mock violin and bow out of cardboard and "plays" the instrument in the privacy of his room.

But gradually, by a subtle process of internalization, he is able to move through the world outside as if he were still in his room. He develops an invisible wall, a protective covering which he can put on or throw off at will, thus enabling him to play himself in the real world, where he feels himself a stranger. Thus, when his friend Alberto is killed, Lou publicly mourns him without anyone's suspecting that he is in mourning: the villagers shrug off Lou's slow walk, bowed head and empty gaze as simply the antics of the child who lives in the slate house. Obviously Lou's odd behavior invites further alienation by the villagers, which in turn prompts him to greater efforts of eccentric role-playing; and so the circular pattern of signal and response between Lou and the normal society around him is established. But these private rituals are also the earliest efforts of the artist (Lou/Divine/Genet), by means of which he is able to displace the real world and create his own:

> Culafroy had a wretched destiny, and it is because of this that his life was composed of those secret acts, each of which is in essence a poem, as the infinitesimal movement of the finger of a Balinese dancer is a sign that can set a world in motion because it issues from a world whose multifarious meaning is unavowable. Culafroy became Divine; he was thus a poem written only for himself, hermetic to whoever did not have the key to it. In short, this is his secret glory.

The other source of solace for Lou is, of course, Alberto, the exotic Corsican, the wily collector of snakes, and, significantly, the first of Lou-Divine's lovers. Like Lou's phantasy world, "Alberto's pants" are a refuge from the hostile world. Homosexuality, as crime will be later, is just another logical step in Lou's inverted evolution—not necessarily because Lou revolts, but because he has simply come to consider himself as excluded from normal human society and, therefore, heterosexuality. Solange, the only girl Lou is ever to be acquainted with, brushes him off with the same casual disdain as do all the other villagers; conversely, Alberto, who is already in the demimonde to which Lou is consigned, welcomes him with impatient arms. Furthermore, Alberto's kisses are sweeter because they are forbidden: they belong to those "secret acts" which will ultimately become the "poem" Lou-Divine.

When Alberto is killed in a knife fight (Lou's love affairs will always be brief and tragic), there is little to hold him to the village, so he runs away. His next appearance is in the inevitable reformatory. But the reformatory is not a hellhole that functions only to transform juvenile delinquents into polished criminals. Repeatedly throughout his writings Genet refers to the reformatory (or "colony") with fondness and nostalgia, often likening it to the Mother whom, in reality, he never knew. It is in the reformatory, among a host of other scruffy waifs, that Lou first experiences any sense of a home. Suddenly, he is like everybody else: his inverted life patterns are the norm:

> Under the hammocks, amidst the magic of these occupations, loves were born, flared up, and died, with all the usual trappings of love: hatred, cupidity, tenderness, consolation, revenge.

Not only homosexuality, but other modes of deviation, particularly crime, now acquire value:

> What made the colony a realm distinct from the realm of the living was the change of symbols and, in certain cases, of values. The colonists had their own dialect, which was closely related to that of the prisons, and hence a particular ethics and politics. The form of government, which was involved with the religion, was the regime of force, protector of Beauty. Their laws are seriously observed.

Soon Lou steals. When caught, and asked why he steals, he answers, as did the youthful Genet, "Because the others thought I was a thief." Again, his action is determined by, is a response to, signals that come to him from without. But now he is in conformity with an external authority (his fellow inmates), though still in opposition to that other, legal-societal authority (here the nuns who run the reformatory). In the colony he takes on definite form and function; henceforth, he will be the homosexual criminal in a world of law-abiding heterosexuals. To be sure, his new identity "depends" on its opposite (and its opposite, as we shall see, depends on it). But what is significant now is that Lou, for the first time, consciously affirms his exile; he does more—he sublimates it into a system of values, a way of life, a kind of religion. The colony is Lou's black communion, a decisive stage in his ultimate "sainthood."

The period immediately following Lou's escape from the reformatory—three years of begging, living out of garbage cans, sleeping in the park—are only glossed over in the novel.[7] It is on Lou's adult years in Paris, between the ages of twenty and thirty, that Genet focuses. Between his escape from the reformatory and his appearance in Montmartre, Lou has somehow metamorphosed into a total faggot-queen now called Divine, in referring to whom Genet hereafter uses the feminine gender. The reader, along with both Genet and Divine, occasionally experiences uncertainty as to whether Lou-Divine is male or female. But in her features, her dress, her physical movements, her attitudes, and especially her way of thinking about herself in relation to men, Divine's "transvestitism" is for the most part convincing.

Hereafter, she will live in Montmartre in a garret overlooking a cemetery. As a male prostitute, her haunts will be wherever she can pick up clients: in homosexual bars, theatres, railroad stations and on the streets. Her friends will be either hoodlum-lovers (Darling Daintyfoot, Our Lady of the Flowers, Seck Gorgui) or other queens (First Communion, Banjo, the Abbess, the Queen of Romania, Mimosa II, Milord the Prince). In her best days, her lovers will be aristocrats and millionaires; in the beginning and in the end, anyone who can pay.

The world that Divine moves in has its own distinct structure and character. The queens meet for tea in the afternoon, either at one another's dens or in the local "gay" cabaret. They dress in "drag." They have frequent closed parties. They are familiar with the intimate details of one another's lives and gossip shamelessly. They vie for the same lovers, at times amicably exchanging them, at other times literally tearing each other's hair out for them. Loves are brief; feckless lovers come and go with the casualness of children at play. Childlike too is the cruelty that lover inflicts on lover, friend on friend, in a world where honor, loyalty, gratitude—the bulwark of the bourgeois moral structure—have never been learned or have long been forgotten:

> Our domestic life and the law of our Homes do not resemble your Homes. We love each other without love. Our homes do not have the sacramental character. Fags are the great immoralists. In the twinkling of an eye, after six years of union, without considering himself attached, without thinking that he was causing pain or doing wrong, Darling decided to leave Divine. Without remorse, only a slight concern that perhaps Divine might refuse ever to see him again.

[7] For a thorough account of these years in Genet's own life, the reader is referred to *The Thief's Journal*.

Domestic bliss is threatened by other quirks of chance: ill-health, brought on by riotous living and physical neglect (Divine dies of consumption at thirty); periodic arrest and imprisonment; sudden death; and always age. An extraordinary premium is placed on youth and beauty, both for the "male" and for the "female," and one is already old at the age of thirty.

Since they have "elected" to be female, they work at their new sex. Hence, they exaggerate, actually parody, the feminine. Their gestures are overdelicate, overrefined; their eyes melt; their bodies undulate when they walk; they affect a lilting purr in their voices, especially when they flirt. Divine makes her first appearance in Paris as follows:

> That evening she was wearing a champagne silk short-sleeved blouse, a pair of blue trousers stolen from a sailor, and leather sandals. On one of her fingers, though preferably on the pinkie, an ulcer-like stone gangrened her. When the tea was brought, she drank it as if she were at home, in tiny little sips (a pigeon), putting down and lifting the cup with her pinkie in the air. Here is a portrait of her: her hair is brown and curly; with the curls spilling over her eyes and down her cheeks, she looks as if she were wearing a cat-o-nine tails on her head. Her forehead is somewhat round and smooth. Her eyes sing, despite their despair, and their melody moves from her eyes to her teeth, to which she gives life, and from her teeth to all her movements, to her slightest acts, and this charm, which emerges from her eyes, unfurls in wave upon wave, down to her bare feet.

The queen bakes pies for her lover, hustles in the streets and gives him her earnings, pets him and fusses over him (Divine ties nosegays around her lover's genitals—she would like to say Mass on his chest); and she is happy if, in return, he beats her. The faggots play only the feminine role in sexual union—that is, they receive the male's discharge, either in the mouth or in the anus; their own penis has no function in the act, viz., it is negated. (It is only after she has satisfied the male that Divine goes to the toilet and finishes herself off by masturbating.)[8] Even their language is distorted to reflect this bizarre parody of the Female: "I'm the Quite-Alone." "I'm the Quite-Persecuted." "I'm the Quite-Fluff-Fluff." "My God, I'm the Quite-Giddy." "I'm the Quite-Quite." "I'm the Q.Q." "I'm a Thrilling Thing."

---

[8] I am using the terms *queen* and *faggot* interchangeably here. They both designate the "female" partner in a sexual relationship between two men. The generic term *homosexual* applies to any kind of sexual activity between people of the same sex. Therefore, a homosexual may be quite masculine. Genet says, "A male that fucks another male is a double male."

"I really am, sure sure sure, the Quite Profligate." "Oh, Ladies, I'm acting like such a harlot." "You know . . . *yoouknow,* I'm the Consumed-with-Affliction."

Of course, femininity is only second nature to the faggots; their biological nature is still male. They are reminded of this when they discharge some bodily function, like shaving and urinating, or when they masturbate. Their basic maleness also leaps out in moments of stress, when they are enraged, for example, or when they are physically attacked by a rival. It can also manifest itself on those infrequent occasions when they become infatuated with a male who is less masculine than themselves, whereupon they imperceptibly begin to emulate the gestures and postures of the domineering male. Thus they must be continually exerting their will to counteract their nature:

> Divine would be fairly strong physically, but she fears the movements of the riposte, because they are virile, and her modesty makes her shy away from the facial and bodily grimaces that effort requires.

Their "sex," then, is an elaborate and precarious mythology that can be exposed at any moment. When, for example, the faggots and queens are summoned to give testimony in a real court of law and must respond to their real names (Mimosa II to "Rene Hirsch," First Communion to "Eugene Marceau," Divine to "Lou Culafroy"), their world, for the moment at least, collapses. "They were reduced to nothing, and that's the best thing that's been done so far."

But despite their biological makeup, the faggots do not embody quintessential masculine attributes—hardness, power, directness, self-containment. Though these qualities can be incorporated in soldiers, sailors, policemen and assorted proletarian men—actually, in any virile male—in Genet's writings they generally find their most splendid expression in the hoodlum, the other major figure in Genet's underground world. The hoodlum is the male lover to the female faggot. To be sure, there are criminals who are not homosexual and vice versa; but since Genet is ultimately writing about himself (and thus converting the external world into a metaphor for himself), the gay world he depicts is scarcely distinguishable from his underworld. Some of his toughest bruisers—pimps, burglars, dope-smugglers, armed robbers, murderers—indulge in homosexuality. Conversely, faggots such as Divine frequently try their hand at various kinds of petty crimes, such as shoplifting or dope-peddling or "rolling" their clients, so that they too spend much of their lives in prison. Within the prison itself, the blending of the two outcasts, criminal and homosexual, is complete.

Genet portrays a variety of hoodlums, ranging from insignificant bums to heroes of mythic proportions. His pantheon of genuine criminals— Pilorge, Weidmann, Angel Sun, Soclay, Snowball, Harcamone—seem to inhabit a distant sphere, which Genet evokes in his dreams and imagination. (We are reminded of Steppenwolf's Immortals.) Though they are generally modeled after "real" people whom he has known or read about in newspapers and true detective magazines, in his writings they are transformed into demigods:

> Already the murderer compels my respect. Not only because he has known a rare experience, but because he has suddenly set himself up as a god, on an altar, whether of shaky boards or azure air. I am speaking to be sure of the conscious, even cynical murderer, who dares take it upon himself to deal death without trying to refer his acts upon some power of a given order, for the soldier who kills does not assume responsibility, nor does the lunatic, nor the jealous man, nor the one who is called an outcast, who, confronted only with himself, still hesitates to behold himself at the bottom of a pit into which, with his feet together, he has—curious prospector—hurled himself with a ludicrously bold leap. A lost man.

Beyond any laws except those which they lay down, they are bold and, if need be, savage; their gestures are precise and deadly, prompted by an independent will embedded somewhere in their loins. Since they are idealizations, they rarely appear as fictional characters per se taking stage-front and discharging a function in the plot of Genet's stories. Genet brings them into *Our Lady of the Flowers* by way of digression, often in the form of lyrical and spontaneous outbursts, or he uses them as a mythic backdrop against which the human drama is played, as if he feared to sully their images with too close, too realistic, a presentation of them.

The underworld people he does focus on in *Our Lady of the Flowers* are, instead, "roughnecks of undistinguished personality, with none of the nobility that comes from heroism." Darling and Our Lady of the Flowers, Divine's lovers, are "hoodlums of the worst sort." Darling, sometimes pimp, sometimes petty crook, but mostly parasite, is vain, trivial, and totally amoral. An unabashed coward, he thinks nothing of betraying friends to pick up money or save himself a beating by the police. He can imitate the "genuine" hoodlums of Chicago and Marseille only in his gestures and mannerisms, just as Genet can reach them only through his dreams. He is a cock-of-the-walk, and stripped of his surface glitter, he would be an empty shell were it not for a few turds inside him that he can never quite eliminate. Our Lady of the Flowers (Danny) unthinkingly strangles an old man in the course of robbing him. Yet he is only an "innocent murderer"; instead of consciously willing his act he confesses, "I didn't do it on purpose." He is somewhat stupid, clumsy and insensitive, and he is easily intimidated by cops and other toughs (with whom, in sexual relations, he assumes the feminine role). Lacking Darling's virility and grand manner (Darling will walk the length of Paris till he finds a toilet in a fashionable hotel so that he can defecate in style), Our Lady's fascination for Genet is, first, the fact that he committed a murder (however contemptible his reasons) and, secondly, his extraordinary good looks.

Our Lady and Darling, in short, are human and pathetic, at times even comical. They are more like Genet himself. To be sure, they commit real crimes and go to jail, but they only *play* at being criminals. The practice of crime is for them a means to something else (to obtain money, to achieve the esteem of their peers, to fill their own nothingness), but it is not a necessity of their being.[9] Like Genet the poet, Ernestine the dreamer, Divine the female impersonator, Darling and Our Lady are fakes, playing out their hoodlum-fantasies.

The fact remains, however, that they do commit crimes and they do go to jail. If crime is only a role, the role at least is "real." Their choice of that role is an irremediable one that cuts them off from society, and though their exile lacks the glamor of Pilorge's and that of the other "authentic" criminals, it is just as complete. For Genet, there is only a thin line between the underworld and society, between prison and the "world of the living." Genet's own "rehabilitation" notwithstanding, once a man crosses into the underworld—and the slightest error in judgement may suffice to propel him there—he rarely leaves it. For an implacable "fatality" (not to be confused with determinism) governs Genet's outcasts, including the "punks." Even Darling experiences this instant, irreversible metamorphosis into the condemned man when he is caught shop-lifting:

---

[9] They are like the misguided Le Franc in *Deathwatch,* who deliberately kills a man in order to earn the reputation of a murderer, only to be called a phony afterwards by the authentic murderer, Green Eyes.

...a new universe instantaneously presented itself to Darling: the
universe of the irremediable. It is the same as the one we were in, with
one peculiar difference: instead of acting and knowing we are acting,
we know we are acted upon. A gaze—and it may be of your own
eyes—has the sudden precise keeness of the extra-lucid, and the order
of this world—seen inside out—appears so perfect in its inevitability
that this world has only to disappear. That's what it does in the
twinkling of an eye. The world is turned inside out like a glove.

Actually, everybody in Genet's novels seems doomed. Faggots soon get
old, lose their looks, and die prematurely from riotous living; hoods are
suddenly hauled off to jail or executed in the bloom of youth. Hence
Genet's characters, like the Absurd Man and the Existentialist, place an
extraordinary emphasis on the present. Their actions are not determined by
long-range objectives or categorical imperatives of any kind, but only by
the pleasure of the moment, the pursuit of which is often frenetic. The
queens—who make a cult of trivia—go into raptures over a novel style of
dress, a spicy piece of gossip or a new "trick"; the thrill of pulling off a
successful crime, and squandering the loot in a brief spending spree, suffices
for their underworld lovers. All of them pamper their senses with drugs or
alcohol or exotic sex practices. And the orgasm—that keenest of all
sensations, and the one that is most certain to be followed by the desired
oblivion—is their Absolute.

This, then, is the world in which Divine lives out the last ten years of
her brief life. Divine, like the earlier Lou, plays her role, but plays it with
more competence and assurance. She is quickly acknowledged by her
sisters to be the most accomplished artist of "high faggotry." Not only
does she master the vocabulary, gestures, voice and dress of the queen; but
she brings to her role more imagination and inventiveness, more style and
grace, than her competitors. She attracts handsomer or richer or tougher
lovers, spends more lavishly (when she has the money), develops a sharper
eye for the beautiful and the bizarre, and puts on a breezier front to the
world. She is the mistress of the flamboyant gesture, who always describes
a wide arc when she removes her handkerchief from her pocket. Even in
her decline, when younger beauties threaten to supplant her as queen of
the Montmartre fairies, she commands respect. This is dramatically
illustrated when, after her pearl tiara falls to the cabaret floor
(foreshadowing her own "fall"), she grandiloquently pulls her bridge

out of her mouth, plants it on her head, and announces, "Dammit all, Ladies, I'll be queen anyhow."

Divine is also more conscious than any of the other "imagined" characters in the novel; therefore like Jean and other underground protagonists, she suffers more intensely. She is especially cognizant of the tragic end that awaits her and her friends. After she passes her peak—her lovers have deserted her, she is quickly losing her looks, she knows she will soon die of consumption—she prepares for her final role, sainthood. God (Genet?) destined her to play this role from the beginning but she resisted it; now that it is inescapable, she plunges herself into it. Thus, as she physically wastes away, she deliberately makes herself unattractive, cutting off her lashes, discarding her elegant mannerisms, and assuming a frozen expression on her face. She begins to practice self-humiliation and self-mortification, adopts a "pale, celestial" voice, and even wears a sackcloth next to her skin. Like the earlier Lou, she begins to withdraw into the "privacy of her glory." To hasten her detachment from the living, she robs and betrays her friends; and to crown her "dehumanization," she commits the most despicable crime she can imagine, a crime that would disgust Genet's ideal hoodlum: she entices a child to fall from a ninth-story balcony to its death. With this act, Divine knows she is morally dead. "What good," she asks herself, "would it do me to be a thousand times good now? How could this inexpiable crime ever be redeemed?"[10]

No doubt Genet parodies religion by canonizing Divine. Divine rejected belief in the substance of religion long ago, when, as Lou Culafroy, she overturned the ciborium in the church. But she retained the form of religion—its structure and hierarchy, its passion and its beauty. "Saintliness" is the highest achievement of the religious life. Divine, committed to the inverse of that life—evil, or the underworld—plays her role with the same integrity and purity. Saintliness for her is the last, climactic gesture in a life concocted out of ritualistic acts (the playing of the phantom violin, the metamorphosis from male to female, the adoration of the god-lover Darling). As a cast-off her choice of underground life is certainly significant. But once she has made that choice, the style of her

[10] Throughout his writings, Genet appears to be fascinated by betrayal. Betrayal is, essentially, the violation of trust and love. It is therefore the most *unhuman* act that humans are capable of. Divine (like Genet, as we shall see later) resolves to separate herself not only from society, but all of humanity as well. Thus in her (and Genet's) inverted ethical system betrayal is "saintly" because it marks the culminating stage of our dehumanization.

life, and not its content, becomes her absolute. Though her life has been sordid and miserable, and steeped in evil, it is a work of art brought to completion. And saintliness is the measure of its perfection.

UNDERGROUND MAN AND
COMMUNISM

Chapter 7

André Malraux: *Man's Fate*
and
Arthur Koestler: *Darkness at Noon*

Although belief in absolutes of any kind is in direct contradiction to underground man, the urge to believe is not. God may be nothing more than a meaningless abstraction for the writers we have taken up after Hesse and Kafka; however, each of them has postulated an ideal—Existentialist action for Sartre, absurdist revolt for Camus, mythmaking for Genet —offering motive for life and action comparable to the impetus provided by faith in God. Yet all of these substitutes reflect the uniqueness of their creators, each of whom stresses the relative, provisional and subjective element of human behavior (and each of whom appears also to be a genius). At the same time, there are innumerable underground men who would escape the plight of their prototype, the hero of *Notes from Underground,* but who have been unable to create their own special style—men who cannot themselves erect that ladder which will provide them egress from underground. Their discontent being inseparable from acute self-preoccupation, it is understandable that they would seek release in a collective God-surrogate, e.g., Marx's dialectical materialism, particularly as it has been implemented in Communism.

Of all mass movements in modern times, none has had so dramatic, widespread and enduring an appeal as Communism. Its attraction for the working multitudes, to whom it promised a "classless" society, is self-evident. But Communism has also repeatedly drawn into its ranks intellectuals from all corners of the world. Many of them come from the proletariat, but most of them, including underground man, were originally from the middle class, the immediate adversary of the Communists. Along with the industrial workers and peasants, the intellectuals were inspired by such obvious Marxist ideals as the equal distribution of wealth, the abolition of social distinctions and class perquisites, and the dignity of the common man. But whereas the proletariat hoped to realize primarily material benefits in the triumph of Communism, the intellectuals—internationally renowned men no less than underground man—saw in it the possibilities of a spiritual rejuvenation as well.

By definition, one cannot be both a Communist and an underground man. But one can renounce underground for Communism (and vice versa), as in fact many actual and potential underground men did. Underground man is not an indifferent cynic: he is enraged at social and political absurdities, which are among the basic reasons why he went underground in the first place. If he withdrew, it was only because he had despaired of finding a rational basis for idealism and a practical program of action, which are precisely what Communism offered him. However, in declaring himself a Communist he made his own leap of faith. Whereas formerly he had been unable to accept God as the First and Final Cause (the point at which his questionings must cease), he now managed to accommodate himself to another absolute: Historical Necessity. He may have been genuinely convinced that his switch to Communism was prompted by a reasoned analysis of history and experience. Or he may have seen it for the act of faith that it really was and yet, in his desperation, been willing to forsake that unbearable intellectual integrity that characterizes underground man. Of course, the genuine underground man could not suppress his intellect very long, and his insistence on honest thought was to bring him, and intellectuals in general, into continual strife with the official Communist Party. (Sartre immediately comes to mind.) But before underground man became disillusioned with the Party, Marx had been a light that beckoned him, at least temporarily, out of his insufferable hole.

Marxist theory, formulated several years before Dostoevsky published his *Notes from Underground,* is essentially Romantic. Like his predecessor Rousseau, Marx argues that the individual by nature is neither "good" nor "bad" but that society corrupts him, the corrupting element being the inequality between one social class and another. Marx maintains that a classless society is not only possible but also inevitable. Of the two remaining historical classes, "bourgeois" and "proletariat," only the proletariat will survive because capitalism, the social organization on which the bourgeoisie depends, is self-destructive. With the "dictatorship of the proletariat," all class distinctions—in effect all "classes"—will have broken down and been supplanted by a condition of universal brotherhood and equality.

But although capitalism is doomed because of its inherent contradictions, it will not just conveniently disappear. There must first be a revolution, if only a "bloodless" one, in which the proletariat delivers a gentle death blow to the moribund bourgeoisie. Therefore, Communism, like the Church Militant several centuries earlier, demanded action and involvement from its adherents. This call to action, in turn, roused the frustrated intellectuals, including underground man, out of their torpor. They no longer had to be passive onlookers purveying harmless ideas while the real business of society was being conducted by the capitalist and his hirelings. They could now write pamphlets, organize cells, infiltrate unions and government and the media, practice espionage, or make proletarian art. And the once isolated underground man could now belong to an organization around which he might structure all his waking hours, drawing support from comrades of similar bent and daily renewing his faith in the ultimate meaning and effectiveness of everything he did.

The major confirmation of Marxist theory in this century was World War I and its aftermath. Those who were not gulled by patriotic slogans were appalled not only by the waste, the stupidity, the corruption and the sheer brutality of that war, but also by its futility. They were convinced that the war "to end war," in fulfillment of Marxist prophecy, would be followed by bigger and bloodier wars as advanced nations maneuvered for more markets and colonies; and that government, the press, the pulpit, the classroom, and the arts could always be manipulated by big business to support these wars. Betrayed by their education and culture, idealists became cynics. Satirists such as Brecht and Shaw excoriated the powers which had spawned the war; Dadaists created "anti-art," on the assumption that traditional art was instrumental in bringing about the war; Surrealists sought escape from decadent society into the personal world of dreams; flappers flouted their parents' morality; and jazz trumpeteers blared out the music of decline. For Lenin and his Bolsheviks it was the time for apocalyptic action, and shortly before the end of the war they responded with the Russian Revolution.

It was not likely that the Bolshevik "experiment" would limit itself to Russia or even Europe. As John Reed noted at the time, the twenty-day Revolution "shook the world." In the half-century since the events of October, 1917, revolution has been fostered in Asia, Africa, the Middle

East and Latin America. The most sensational and successful Marxist revolution in recent years has been, of course, Castro's overthrow of the Batista regime in Cuba. But the earliest and most significant transplantation of Communism outside Russia took place in China, beginning with the founding of the Chinese Communist Party in 1921 and culminating with Mao Tse Tung's expulsion of Chiang Kai-shek from mainland China in 1949.

Communism in China, of course, is different from its Russian counterpart. In China the peasants played a more crucial role than did the proletariat, and land reform continued to be a major cause of turmoil from the initial revolution of 1911 to the total triumph of Communism in 1949. Colonialism, another source of oppression in China, never existed in modern Russia. For more than a century, from the Opium Wars to Mao's victory in 1949, China was systematically gouged and, in varying degrees, dominated by foreign powers. Besides engaging the Chinese people in open warfare, these countries succeeded in pitting Chinese against Chinese, even worker against worker. Finally, in consequence of this internal divisiveness, the "revolution" dragged on for forty years. The overthrow of the Manchu dynasty in 1912 was followed by civil war, first between the warlords and the Kuomintang and then between the Kuomintang and the Chinese Communists. Communist supremacy was also postponed by the protracted Sino-Japanese War and by direct American assistance to the Kuomintang to fight the Communists after World War II.

MAN'S FATE

Man's Fate, by André Malraux, deals ostensibly with the Shanghai Uprising of 1927 and with its immediate aftermath: in the first half of the novel, a coalition of the Communists and Chiang Kai-shek's Kuomintang, or National, army smashes the major force of the contending warlords; in the second half, with the aid of Western business interests and the Chinese bourgeoisie and the very warlords that he earlier fought, Chiang turns against his erstwhile Communist allies and suppresses, at least temporarily, the Communist movement in China. Thus Chiang, originally the hope of the masses, succeeds in consolidating his power but in doing little else. On the one side, foreign cartels in league with the rich Chinese bourgeoisie still thrive, except that now, instead of paying token tribute to insecure emperors and adventurist generals, they have allied themselves with a strong, central government. On the other side, the poor, who comprise most of the population, are still wretched: land reform is as remote as ever; there is widespread unemployment and gross exploitation of those who are employed; literal hunger is rampant throughout China. Accompanying the economic distress is a breakdown in morale (Confucianism being of little avail). Shanghai is depicted as a Babylon whose fall is forestalled only by the triumph of Chiang Kai-shek. Unscrupulous Western expatriates and underworld natives engage in smuggling and other illegal enterprises. All-night cabarets along the quays and the foreign concessions do a booming business; they are packed with prostitutes whose ranks are continually growing; opium is almost as much a staple as rice; and bribery is the unspoken rule in all areas of society. Although there is hope for a new order in the beginning of the novel, in the end the predominant moods are distrust, fear and despair.

Malraux is unequivocal about the need for revolution in China in the Twenties. But *Man's Fate,* like his other novels, is always more than political. If in such novels as *Man's Fate* and *Man's Hope* he espoused the Communists' cause, it was because he believed at the time of writing them that the Communists promised what has always been Malraux's primary concern: the quality and dignity of the individual, without which there can be no healthy society. Sometime after the publication of these novels he said:

> It's a matter of profound indifference to any of us whether a man is a Communist, an anti-Communist, a liberal, or anything else, because the only real problem is to know, above these structures, in what form we can re-create man![1]

The author does in fact pursue his quest of regenerate man by other routes than Communism in such subsequent volumes as *The Walnut Trees of*

[1] Quoted in Pierre Galante, *Malraux,* New York, 1971, p. 176. Throughout the Twenties and Thirties Malraux openly allied himself with the Communists because they, in his opinion, were the only force actively opposed to colonialism in the Far East and to Fascism in Europe. But Malraux today would certainly qualify his advocacy of Communism. Along with his friend and chief, General de Gaulle, he supported the Algerian independence movement against the French colonialists, but he has hardly been sanguine about Russia's imperialistic encroachments since World War II.

Altenburg and *The Voices of Silence*. Malraux's political views are subservient
to his ethics, which in turn derive from fundamental assumptions that he
makes about the nature of man. Therefore, before we turn to the role of
Communism in such earlier novels as *Man's Fate*, we should examine his
overall conception of man, which has remained constant in his life and art
even after he abandoned his alliance with the Communists.

Beneath its parallels to Marxism, Malraux's philosophy resembles the
thought of Albert Camus, much of whose theory of the absurd he was
expounding several years before Camus. Whatever its positive potential,
man's "fate" or "condition" (*La Condition Humaine*) is inseparable from sickness, suffering and, most absurdly of all, death. In former times, man was
able to reconcile himself to his mortality because he saw himself as a vital
unit in a cosmic scheme which gave meaning both to his life and death.
With the emergence of individualism in the Renaissance, there followed
the cleavage between man and his creator and the disbelief in the essential
oneness of all things: man was an accident, a mere intrusion in an
indifferent universe. This process of alienation, says Malraux, reached its
climax for Western man at the end of the nineteenth century (coinciding
with the appearance of underground man) and thereafter spread, in
modified form, to the Orient. In *The Voices of Silence*, Malraux writes:

> What Christian culture was discarding was more than one or another
> of its values and something even more vital than faith; it was the
> notion of Man orientated towards Being—who was soon to be
> replaced by the man who was capable of being swayed by ideas and
> acts; value was being disintegrated into a plurality of values. What
> was disappearing from the Western world was the Absolute.[2]

Thus with Sartre, Malraux sees modern man as having rejected the
Absolute for isolated "ideas" and "acts" which are divorced from Being.
Consequently, he experiences *anguish*. Anguish is not simply one's
awareness of individual responsibility: it is the prerational apprehension of
his total condition as a human, with all its limitations; or, as Malraux
defines it in *Man's Fate*, "the consciousness of his own fatality, from which
all fears are born, even the fear of death. . . ."[3] In Malraux's earlier novels
(*The Conquerors, The Royal Way*), his heroes are conscious only of the

[2] *The Voices of Silence*, tr. Stuart Gilbert, New York, 1953, p. 481.
[3] André Malraux, *Man's Fate*, tr. Haakon Chevalier, New York, 1934. Subsequent quotations from *Man's Fate* are from this edition.

absurdity of the human condition. In subsequent works, beginning with *Man's Fate,* they are also able to tap its beauty and nobility.

In *Man's Fate,* the absurd takes many forms: contradiction, miscalculation, unexpected twists of fate. Invariably, however, it results in suffering, not just of individuals but of man in general. Hence Malraux focuses on a variety of people and a correspondingly wide range of human miseries: sickness, age, physical pain, hunger, bereavment, loneliness, humiliation and dying; in addition, these normal vicissitudes are aggravated by anxiety and uncertainty over the civil war that is raging in the streets (one cannot escape the persistent smell of corpses). For many of the characters, being human is poor defense against the strains and shocks to which that humanness is subject, and all of them, even the strongest, feel helplessness at one time or another. Malraux underscores this point through his spokesman, Gisors: "It is very rare for a man to be able to endure—how shall I say it—his condition, his fate as a man." Therefore, everyone in the novel seeks to free himself of his human condition and achieve the inviolability of God. Anticipating Sartre's analysis of bad faith, Gisors describes this yearning as follows:

> To be more than a man, in a world of men. To escape man's fate. . . .
> Not powerful: all powerful. The visionary disease, of which the will
> to power is only the intellectual justification, is the will to godhead:
> every man dreams of being god.

The central event of *Man's Fate,* the Shanghai Uprising, functions as a crucial catalyst to all of the characters. Their involvement in or reaction to it seals their separate fates, forcing each of them into lucid awareness of the meaning of his past actions and the future course of his life. One can be simply an innocent victim who gets in the way of a stray bullet. But as Gisors points out in self-recrimination, one's end is generally the logical result of the way he has lived:

> One can fool life for a long time, but in the end it always makes us
> what we were intended to be. Every old man is a confession, believe
> me, and if old age is usually so empty it is because the men were
> themselves empty and had managed to conceal it.

Malraux is not a total determinist. Like Sartre and Camus, he insists that while we cannot determine everything that literally happens to us, we alone are responsible for its moral value. So each of the characters in *Man's Fate* is held up in judgment according to how he copes with the "conditions" of his existence.

Against Malraux's measure, most of the personages in the novel are faulty in one degree or another. In their reactions to anguish, they hate, turn to vice, become cruel or egocentric, or simply withdraw. But these escapes from dread are self-defeating. Vice and cruelty only add to man's initial misfortune; withdrawal and egotism only intensify what is perhaps its key component, isolation. In contrast to these unredeemed figures (Gisors, Clappique, Ferral) are the Communists such as Katov and, especially, Kyo. They are the only ones in the novel dedicated to a cause which transcends them as individuals and which, in principle, is directed to the improvement of the human condition in general. Working in unity instead of isolation, they alone cope successfully with the absurd, even if they die in the struggle. People such as Ch'en, May and Hemmelrich— marginal Communists whose motives include hate, revenge or the desire to kill for the sake of killing—are really more akin to the first group of characters; for Malraux endorses only those Communists who are prompted by the highest, humanitarian principles.

One of the most impressive failures in the novel is Old Gisors. He is the Marxist theoretician who has inspired the young revolutionaries, including his son Kyo, to see in Marxist activism the means by which they can reconstruct a decadent China and effect, in themselves and their down-trodden countrymen, a sense of dignity. When the novel opens, however, the sixty-year-old former professor is uninvolved in the revolutionary ferment he helped to create, though he has lost neither his incisive intellect nor the respect of his former students. He now limits his "activities" to conversation with friends and pure contemplation, both made bearable by five pellets of opium every day. His sole link with the current scene is Kyo—his "arm" and his "will" in the world—indeed, his only reason for living. Ironically, Kyo and Gisors' other disciples, being actively engaged in the revolution from which Gisors has detached himself, are moving away from him in exact proportion as they are involved in it and he is not. When Kyo dies because of his Communist commitments, Old Gisors succumbs totally to his opium addiction, rejecting not only entreaties that he plunge himself into the revolution and thus vindicate his son's death, but also the will to live itself.

But Gisors was obsessed with death long before his son died. Besides being the Marxist theoretician in the novel, he is Malraux's most articulate interpreter of the absurd. Since consciousness must ultimately be consciousness of anguish, Gisors, who thinks more than the others, is more acutely aware of the folly of human existence. He sees death everywhere, for which Marxism offers little comfort. He confesses in the end:

> Marxism has ceased to live in me. In Kyo's eyes it was a will, wasn't it? But in mine, it is a fatality, and I found myself in harmony with it because my fear of death was in harmony with fatality.

Yet at the conclusion of the novel he waits for death, indeed wills it (that "deadly parasite in a secret recess of his being"), as he caresses his opium pipe and contemplates, in disdain and cynicism, the teeming life around him. Thus Gisors' contemplation leads him to the point of embracing rather than fighting the absurd; of having conceived the means of combatting it (i.e., Marxist activism) only to leave their use to others. Consistent with underground man, he allows his intellect to become his curse.

If Gisors seeks release from anguish, Clappique attempts to deny its existence. Remnant of the vanished European aristocracy, "dealer in antiques, opium and smuggled wares," an elegant clown who invents fabulous tales for the amusement of prostitutes, Baron de Clappique is committed to nothing. If he takes part in the revolution (the side being unimportant), he does so only as an actor playing one of his numerous roles. Like Genet, Jean Baptiste Clamence and Underground Man, he is characterized as a "mythomaniac," who concocts "whole biographies" for himself and who involves himself in his myths with greater relish than he has for reality. Clappique thinks of himself as a dead man. Yet when he is threatened with literal death, he desperately clings to life. To escape Chiang Kai-shek's police, he stows away on a ship disguised as a sailor —another role!

Denying self and the irritations of responsibility, Clappique carries on a running flirtation with chance. This is best illustrated when he lingers at the roulette table instead of keeping an appointment with Kyo. If he sees Kyo, the latter will provide him the money he needs to leave Shanghai; he, on his part, has information that is vital to Kyo. But Clappique prefers to risk both his and Kyo's life on the roulette table. He is fascinated by the capriciousness and the absurdity of his decision. On the one hand, he sees in roulette a simile for his life: fate is the wheel and he is both the ball and the stake. (The fact that Kyo is also one of the stakes intensifies his frenzy.) On the other hand, he experiences a momentary, if perverted, sense of power, for he knows that he is deliberately gambling with two lives. Paradoxically, Clappique's one deliberate assertion of self consists in handing that self over to fate.

But Clappique is only too aware of his role-playing—his suppression of his real self is always a conscious effort. Hence, he does feel anguish; and to the extent that he wastes his life in denying it, he is also ashamed. Latent in the man is a sense of human dignity and worth, which neither his heavy drinking nor his hectic sexuality nor his mythomania can ever annihilate (Gisors thinks he should try opium). For all his urbane detachment, he is, like Jean Baptiste Clamence, a tormented man, torn between the impulse for authentic being and the desire simply to fade away. When, for example, he has lost his money at roulette and failed to deliver the information that would save Kyo's life, he is a moral wreck. Language at last fails the ordinarily eloquent Baron; so, standing before the mirror, he resorts to dumb show to express his self-loathing:

> And immediately, as if he had found a way of expressing directly in all its intensity the torment which words were not adequate to translate, he began to make faces, transforming himself into a monkey, an idiot, a terrified person, an apoplectic, into all the grotesques that a human face can express. This no longer sufficed: he used his fingers, drawing out the corners of his eyes, enlarging his mouth for the toad face of the man-who-laughs.

Gisors and Clappique disengage themselves in order to cope with anguish. Ferral, on the other hand, suffers precisely to the extent that he does not determine his own destiny. He is a brilliant, ruthless "empire builder" who, like the protagonists of Malraux's earlier novels (the "conquerors"), despoils the Orient in order to shore up his fortunes in his native Europe. He is head of the Franco-Asiatic Consortium, a complex cartel which involves numerous governments, international bankers and merchants throughout the world and which determines the economic condition of millions of people, especially in Asia, the primary source of cheap labor. Politically, then, he is clearly to the "right," prepared to support whoever protects his financial empire. In the beginning of the novel, he backs the warlord government against the coalition of Chiang Kai-shek and the Communists. With the imminent victory of the latter, he nimbly shifts his support to Chiang's bourgeois Kuomintang, since the Communists are obviously his natural enemy.

Ferral seeks wealth because he aspires to political power in France. But his will to power is evident in every facet of his life. Aspiring to a perverted form of Nietzsche's Superman (which Malraux considers a major malady of modern Western man), Ferral has a compulsion to dominate, to possess "the means of coercing men and things." Like Sartre's man of bad faith, he approaches the world as if it were unshaped wax waiting for him to imprint his own figure upon it. Since his lust for power is not inspired by any great idea or vision, it is destructive. He takes pleasure in humiliating and intimidating people—in denying them their dignity: he compels Geisha girls to undress without their first singing or dancing; he mocks the mentality of his mistresses and tries to induce "Christian shame" in them when he makes love to them (insisting the light be kept on so that he can read, in the gratification written on their faces, proof of their degradation); he forces dependents to violate fundamental codes of conduct; he belittles the efforts of subordinates; he addresses his Chinese servants as "boy." With the pain that he persistently inflicts on his fellow men, who know suffering enough without Ferral, he is a formidable servant of the absurd.

But Ferral is also a victim of the absurd. As Sartre subsequently pointed out, bad faith is self-defeating. Ferral is dependent on the people he humiliates—dependent, indeed, on their humiliation. For he can neither enjoy nor be certain of his power unless it is reflected back to him from his victims:

> He derived his pleasure from putting himself in the place of the other, that was clear: of the other, compelled; compelled by him. In reality he never went to bed with anyone but himself, but he could do this only if he were not alone . . . yes, his will to power never achieved its object, lived only by renewing it. . . .

If, as eventually happens, people do not give him this satisfaction, he goes into a rage or suffers anguish. Yet he is most attracted to those who are least likely to submit to him, just as Nietzsche's Superman admired his deadliest enemy because the latter was his greatest challenge. Thus Ferral receives his first serious jolt in the novel when he is rejected by his mistress Valerie, an attractive woman with a will equal to his own. What he finds most alluring in her is her independence, which whets his appetite for dominance; yet it is this independence, fortified by her resentment of the male sex (particularly the Ferrals), which makes it impossible for him to possess her.

A more devastating defeat for Ferral is the collapse of the Consortium.

In a conversation with Gisors, he declaims, in ringing Sartrean cadences:

> A man is the sum of his actions, of what he has *done*, of what he can
> do. Nothing else. I am not what such and such an encounter with a
> man or woman may have done to shape my life; I am my roads. . . .

But Gisors quietly cuts him short with the reply, "The roads had to be built." Ferral is the primary force behind the Consortium, but he is not the only one. In spite of his excellent management of it, its actual survival depends on his credits. These, in turn, are determined solely by the natural richness of his rubber plantations and the inflated price of rubber, both of which are beyond his control. When the price of rubber drops and he is unable to obtain necessary credits, his financial conglomerate comes tumbling down. Thus Ferral is not the nonpareil he so desperately needs to believe he is. For all his delusions of infallibility, he too suffers from man's fate.

Alone, cynical and proud, even as his last petition is being turned down by men he has always scorned, Ferral would surely be one of the most pathetic characters in the novel if the reader could muster up more sympathy for him. His ideal being himself in the mode of Nietzsche's Superman, the disintegration of the Consortium leaves him with nothing. Having lived only for himself, he cannot draw on human support to cushion his fall. Nor is his loss justified or redeemed by a principle that transcends his naked ego (he has always considered it a "stupidity characteristic of the human race" to sacrifice one's life for an idea). His egotism, no less than Gisors' opium and Clappique's mythomania, is a futile escape from anguish.

Although the limitations of Gisors, Clappique and Ferral tend to set off the virtues of some of the Communists, Malraux hardly recommends all of them as models to be emulated. Communism, like intellect and power and mythmaking, should ultimately be only an instrument in the service of man; but like all tools, it can be abused. May and Hemmerlich, for example, see in Communism the means of avenging the deaths of their loved ones. But neither of them puts Communism to more perverted uses than the terrorist Ch'en, for whom it becomes the justification of murder for its own sake.

There is nothing extraordinary in Ch'en's initial attraction to Communism. Poverty alone could have impelled him in that direction, as it did thousands of other Chinese peasants and workers in the Twenties. In addition, Communism answered to several spiritual needs of this Oriental underground man. Awkward and shy, lonely, extremely sensitive, convinced of his unworthiness yet seething with inner rage, this potential idealist longed for an absolute. Early in his education, Ch'en hectically subjected himself to the Kierkegaardian teachings of a guilt-ridden Lutheran pastor, the first of Ch'en's gurus. But since Christianity ran counter to his suppressed anger, and Christian meditation to his urge for involvement in the China outside the cloister, religion left him unsatisfied, particularly since an extremist such as Ch'en could not content himself with anything short of saintliness. Owing to the influence of the morbid pastor, however, Christianity did manage to magnify his already considerable sense of guilt: like Kafka's Judaism, it transformed his personal self-contempt into a generalized conviction of the fallen state of man. It was therefore easy for Ch'en, under the tutelage of his new teacher Gisors, to switch to Communism. Besides providing him with an ideology as total and absorbing as Christianity, it offered him opportunities for immediate action, the results of which would be more evident than the otherworldly compensations of Christianity. Furthermore, it gave him a sense of dignity: the hateful foreign capitalist, and not a depraved Ch'en or sinful mankind, was the enemy.

But Communism begins to lose its allure for Ch'en when, with the first political execution he commits, he discovers joy in murder. In the moment when his first victim expires, he is intoxicated, purged of doubts and anguish; he feels the ecstasy of the mystic transcending himself. Thereafter, terrorism becomes his obsession, beyond will and reason. He elevates murder to a cult, to something more than religion, to the

> ... meaning of life.... The complete possession of oneself. Total. Absolute. To know. Not to be looking, looking, always, for ideas, for duties.

Always a solitary man, Ch'en widens the gap between himself and his fellows by his passion for death instead of life; and with every man he kills, he moves further away from his comrades. The Communist Party, with its discipline and institutionalized structure, becomes distasteful to him. Murder for the Party is only an expedience serving some distant end; for Ch'en it is an absolute to be seized here and now. Possessed of this single truth, he scorns obedience to his superiors. Thus when they prohibit the assassination of Chiang Kai-shek, Ch'en knows he must go his own way:

> If it's a question of killing Chiang Kai-shek, I know. As for this fellow Vologin, it's all the same to him, I guess; but for him, instead of

murder, it's obedience. For people who live as we do there must be a
certainty. For him carrying out orders is sure, I suppose, as killing is
for me. Something *must* be sure. Must be.

Ch'en has not entirely lost sight of the initial ideals for which he joined
the Party: Chiang Kai-shek is still the enemy. Ch'en can also adduce sound
political reasons for the assassination of Chiang and for terrorism in
general. But when he determines to make of himself a human bomb and
plunge himself before Chiang's car, demanding at the same time that his
friends join him in this hara-kiri, he goes beyond politics and revolution.
Killing Chiang along with himself, he hopes to fraternally merge with his
erstwhile enemy in a frenzied apotheosis. His self-immolation is to be his
last, twisted gesture; the climax and vindication of his life; the single
personal achievement that he can believe in. Politically, Ch'en's death is
futile, for the car before which he throws himself is not Chiang's. But we
doubt that Ch'en would be too disappointed were he to know that he failed
to take Chiang with him. His suicide is ultimately a Dionysian celebration
of death for its own sake. Like Ferral's lovemaking (and Genet's mastur-
bation), it is the supreme act of egoism which manages to "join him to
himself in a dizzy embrace." Yet if death is his personal victory, it is also the
triumph of the absurd—nothing is more absurd than death. Ironically,
having started out as the most tormented victim of the absurd, Ch'en ends
his life embracing it like a lover.

The ultimate futility of Gisors, Clappique, Ferral and Ch'en highlights
the nobility of Kyo and Katov. Kyo and Katov owe much of their
grandeur to their unflinching devotion to the Communist cause. It enables
them to die with a heroism that is impossible for underground man. Katov
is perhaps more thoroughly dedicated to the Party, his own identity being
indistinguishable from it. He never questions its wisdom; he does not
concern himself with matters not directly related to it. Although some
brief and dark hints are made about his personal life before the novel opens,
he is actually revealed to us only in pursuit of his political ends; what
personal anguish he feels is effectively sublimated in revolution (Gisors
thinks revolution is Katov's addiction). Thus Katov is more limited, more
impersonal, more removed from the reader than is Kyo. Kyo is capable of
going beyond politics, his personal involvements being scarcely less significant than his political activities. More sensitive and self-conscious than
Katov (and just as capable of action), having more of Gisors' incisive
intellect and far-ranging curiosity, he ponders his identity and his destiny
not just as a Communist but as a total human. The oppression of the

masses, as hateful to him as to Katov, is for Kyo only one manifestation of the absurd, and his Communist commitment only one weapon with which to combat it.

For Kyo as for Camus, the absurd on the simplest level is any contradiction between expectation and reality. Throughout the novel he is continually confronted with the unexpected: he is shocked when he hears on the phonograph a strange voice–his own–causing him to wonder for the first time how he intuits himself, how others perceive him, and who he really is; he is jarred when his wife casually informs him that she has just slept with another man, in spite of the fact that both she and he, who love each other profoundly, explicitly agreed that each was to have complete sexual freedom; he is plunged into despair when the Central Committee of the Communist Party orders him to turn over the guns to Chiang (only to rescind that order immediately after Kyo executes it).

Kyo is saddened by each of these experiences; but given the unique circumstances of his upbringing–his lifelong witness to the plight of the coolie, the Westerner's inbred scorn for the Oriental, his father's Marxist teachings–he sees capitalism in general and colonialism in particular as the main source of misery in the China of the Twenties. Unlike many intellectuals, Kyo turned to Communism out of a profound personal identification with the oppressed masses:

> His life had a meaning, and he knew what it was: to give to each of these men whom famine, at this very moment, was killing off like a slow plague, the sense of his own dignity. He belonged with them: they had the same enemies. A half-breed, an outcast, despised by the white men and even more by the white women, Kyo had not tried to win them: he had sought and had found his own kind. "There is no possible dignity, no real life for a man who works twelve hours a day without knowing why he works." That work would have to take on a meaning, become a faith. Individual problems existed for Kyo only in his private life.

Thus Communism for Kyo is not just a self-serving attempt to escape personal anguish, as opium is for Gisors, power for Ferral, mythomania for Clappique, and murder for Ch'en. Nor is it simply unreflecting subservience to the Party, as it is for Katov. Kyo is a Communist because he hates any form of inhumanity: his sympathy for the downtrodden is reflected in his daily acts, in his gentleness, his generosity, his compassion. His *Communism,* then, is a form of human *communion,* as spiritual in its essence as that of the Christian saints, yet inspired by living men and dedicated to the improvement of this world. Kyo, like Camus' Rebel, is the exemplary man because he seeks to transform the human environment in which the absurd thrives.

To the extent that he can improve the economic conditions in China, Kyo removes the purely external obstacles to human dignity. But even though he falls short of his goal, the attempt in itself is an affirmation of the individual Kyo. It is Gisors who, having himself succumbed to the vice of passivity, has taught Kyo that ". . . ideas were not to be thought, but lived," and that "Marxism is not a doctrine, it is a will." Being human, Kyo must suffer: the bizarre miscalculations of the Central Committee, for example, cost him his life, thus curtailing his efforts both as a Communist and as a man. At the same time, however, his death marks his personal triumph. Since Communism is the idea he has freely chosen of himself, his death invests both it and himself with the highest possible meaning: he can do no more than die for it. Kyo takes comfort in this conviction a few moments before he dies:

> He had fought for what in his time was charged with the deepest meaning and the greatest hope. . . . What would have been the value of a life for which he would not have been willing to die?

Another reason why Kyo's death is an "exalted act" is that he dies with those whom he has loved. Contrary to the solitary Ch'en, he derives support from the other condemned prisoners. ("It is easy to die when one does not die alone.") Moments before his death he feels himself a mute participant in a kind of collective mysticism. Indeed, he is aware that the community of the condemned within the prison walls is linked with multitudes of comrades and sympathizers who have escaped Chiang's purge and for whom the Kyos and Katovs would soon be martyrs:

> . . . wherever men labor in pain, in absurdity, in humiliation, they were thinking of doomed men like these, as believers pray; and, in the city, they were beginning to love these dying men as though they were already dead. . . . In all of the earth that this last night covered over, this place of agony was no doubt the most weighted with virile love.

Besides giving value to his own life, then, Kyo's death enables his cause to outlive him; and through his identification with the movement, something of him lives on after his literal death. Whether and to what extent Kyo's dream of social justice ever materializes, man will still be confronting the absurd, which is inseparable from his condition. In contrast to most of the characters in the novel, however, Kyo has done the little that he can do in this age-old struggle, and therein is his glory.

Malraux's bias in *Man's Fate* is, of course, unmistakable: in the Asia of the Twenties, colonialism is an unmitigated evil which only Communism can destroy. This unchallenged assumption determines Malraux's treatment of the various characters in the novel. The Communists, and only the Communists, are admirable; all of the other characters are faulted in one degree or another—Chiang Kai-shek, indeed, is a one-dimensional villain out of melodrama. Human dignity is Malraux's absolute in the novel, but nowhere does he question the right of the Communists to deprive the enemy of his dignity and nowhere does he present the latter's view of the subject sympathetically. On the other hand, the Communists, whose cause is simply presumed to be noble, are capable at worst of only strategic errors.

A case in point is Moscow's directive that the Chinese Communists hand over their guns to Chiang Kai-shek rather than engage him in an armed struggle. Moscow's reasoning, in the novel, is that while a showdown with the Kuomintang and the Communists is inevitable, at the moment Chiang is too strong to be challenged. Kyo, while obeying that order, argues that thousands of workers and peasants, with or without arms, are ready to give battle to Chiang and that, in any event, there can never be any compromise with him since he is bent on smashing Communism in China. When Chiang begins systematically to exterminate the Chinese Communists, the Central Committee in Moscow realizes its mistake and, when it is too late, countermands its original order. For Malraux, the Party's error was tragic enough, but it was only an error. For other historians, notably Leon Trotsky, it had more sinister overtones. According to Trotsky, Stalin restrained the Chinese Communists because he had decreed that China should first have a successful bourgeois, "democratic" revolution led by Chiang and only afterwards a proletarian revolution to overthrow the Kuomintang. But Moscow deliberately kept the mass of its Chinese allies ignorant of its long-term strategy, for which they subsequently paid with their lives. Hence, Trotsky concludes, Stalin actually betrayed the Chinese Revolution.[4]

[4] See Trotsky's interpretation of Stalin's role in China, including Trotsky's specific criticism of Malraux, in Leon Trotsky, *Problems of the Chinese Revolution,* New York, 1962, 2nd edition, pp. 267-293. See also Ignazio Silone's explicit endorsement of Trotsky's position in *The God That Failed,* ed. Richard Crossman, New York, 1949, p. 107-108, and George Moseley's implicit confirmation of it in his *China Since 1911,* New York, 1968, p. 55.

Stalin's "error" in China points up the inevitable dissension between individual Communists and the ruling hierarchy of the Party. In the zeal of idealism, converts had no difficulty swearing initial allegiance, but in time they found it increasingly difficult to accommodate themselves to the Party's amorality. Politburo decisions, they saw, were at repeated variance not only with their personal morality but also with the professed ideals of Communism itself. They were repelled, for example, by the extermination of the kulaks in the Twenties; the carnival of the Moscow trials (including Trotsky's execution), the support of Mussolini against Ethiopia, and the Stalin-Hitler pact in the Thirties; the ruthless suppression of the Hungarian uprising in the Fifties; and countless other instances of duplicity and brutality. Stalin's determination to strengthen Russia, even at the expense of the worldwide Communist movement, was especially repugnant to Western idealists dreaming of universal brotherhood. And they took little solace in the official attitude that some distant historical end (never clearly defined or fixed) would somehow justify the means used in the present, and that morality (as Western liberals understood it) was only "bourgeois" in origin and therefore irrelevant.

No less distasteful to the intellectual was the undisguised anti-intellectualism in the Communist Party, engendered primarily by Stalin after Lenin's death and continuing unabated into the present. Again, in his initial zeal, the intellectual humbled himself before the shibboleth of the "worker" (in effect, the bureaucrat) and willingly submitted to Party indoctrination. But for the genuine intellectual, and particularly underground man (whose obsession for inquiry knows no limits), the deliberate denial of his own judgment became increasingly difficult to make. He was too intelligent, too informed, not to see chinks in the presumed infallibility of the Communist elite. Imagine Communist biologists (including the English Nobel Laureate, J. B. S. Haldane) being told that they must renounce Mendel for Lysenko, not because of experimental evidence, but because of Party edict!

But if there was a single, inviolable rule in the Party, it was undoubtedly total submission of the individual. The concept of individuality was alien to Party structure. Like an army in the field, the Party was most effective when each of its component parts worked in perfect accord under a central command. Hence, absolute obedience was essential: "egoism," "factionalism" and "deviationism" were cardinal errors calling for swift correction. Intellectuals, particularly in the West, soon learned that giving up their freedom was not so easy as they had imagined, for their heritage was basically democratic and liberal. Even Dostoevsky's Underground Man, who lived in czarist Russia, absorbed much of this influence. He denounced Chernyshevsky, as we have seen, not because the latter was an intellectual but because his intellectualism was so shoddy; and though Underground Man bemoaned his excessive freedom, he was unable, or unwilling, to relinquish it.

While revolt among intellectuals was inevitable, actual defection from the Party was extremely painful. Generally, the Party would attempt to lead the recalcitrant back into the fold; but once convinced that he was beyond redemption, it read him out of the movement and, to insure his lasting damnation, branded him with such tags as "counterrevolutionary," "class-collaborationist," "agent provocateur," "smuggler of reaction," "incipient Trotskyite," "petty bourgeois degenerate" and "bastard intellectual." To the countless ex-Communists for whom Communism had once been an all-consuming faith, this ritual was not very amusing. Actually, it was no less tragic for them than excommunication had been for the Christian believer a thousand years earlier. Their commitment being total, when they were ousted from the Party they were left with nothing.

Nonetheless, intellectuals the world over dropped out of the Communist Party, the roll of illustrious defectors being almost as impressive as the list of initial converts. Excluding the large-scale splintering of international Communism (e.g., the breaking away of China, Rumania and Yugoslavia from Russian dominance) and the abortive uprisings in Poland, Hungary and Czechoslovakia, revolt has been limited primarily to America and Western Europe, where one is relatively safe from extreme Party vengeance. Recently, however, the Russian bureaucracy has been challenged by its own native sons, including such prominent writers as Alexander Solzhenitsyn and Andrei Sinyavsky and the renowned biochemist Jaures Medvedev. Their dissent is especially irksome to the Soviet government not only because it continues in spite of harsh repression (for instance, the consignment of dissidents to labor camps and "mental" hospitals), but also because it is regularly leaked out to the rest of the world.[5]

---

[5] By February of 1972, the twenty-seventh issue of the monthly magazine *Chronicle of Current Events,* which is critical of the present regime, had been smuggled out of Russia.

DARKNESS AT NOON

Intellectuals are articulate. Their disaffection with the Communist Party, whether they be "card-carrying" members or "fellow travelers," is bound to find its way into literature. Of the innumerable exposés of the Party in the past half-century, however, the classic is still Arthur Koestler's *Darkness at Noon* (1941), just as *Man's Fate* is probably the best novel written in support of it. The period between the publication of these two novels corresponds, roughly, with Koestler's own very active membership in the Party, a career that he abruptly terminated on that day in 1938, bitter for both Koestler and Malraux, when the "swastika was hoisted on Moscow airport in honor of Ribbentrop's arrival...."[6] Although Koestler's literal experience with the Party is not the subject of *Darkness at Noon*, he does depict the agonizing process by which his own initial enchantment with Communism turned ultimately into anger and disillusionment.

Darkness at Noon is actually based on the Moscow Trials of 1936-1938. The Trials marked Stalin's total victory over his erstwhile Bolshevik comrades-in-arms (Trotsky, Bukharin, Zinoviev, Kamenev, et al.) in a contest for power beginning with Lenin's death in 1924. By 1936 Stalin's enemies had long since ceased to be a threat; but to solidify public opinion in support of his dictatorship, he had them brought to trial for treason. Bukharin was one of those who publicly "confessed"; Trotsky not only maintained his innocence but denounced the Trials as a travesty. Nonetheless, all were found guilty and executed, including Trotsky, who was assassinated in Mexico shortly after the Trials.

The protagonist of the novel is the old Bolshevik Rubashov. Although in certain conspicuous details he is patterned after an amalgam of Trotsky and Bukharin, he is representative of that whole group of revolutionaries who clustered around Lenin in the early days of the Revolution. In contrast to the boorish Stalin (No. 1 in the novel), they are urbane and worldly (Rubashov grew up on an estate), intellectual as well as activist, combining revolutionary zeal with the highest attainments of the bourgeois culture which they have overthrown. They are thus cognizant of two worlds. Still retaining vestiges of the humanistic values of their childhood,

[6] Arthur Koestler, in *The God That Failed,* ed. Richard Crossman, New York, 1949, p. 74.

but religiously suppressing them in the service of Communism, they are complex men who have fallen into increasing disfavor with the Party (actually with No. 1). Suspicious of intellectuals from the outset, and seeing in them now the last threat to his dictatorship, No. 1 has succeeded in liquidating all but Rubashov and one or two others of the old guard. *Darkness at Noon* begins with Rubashov's arrest.

Thus while Kyo becomes an outlaw because of his commitment to Communism, Rubashov becomes one because of his defection from it. No. 1, and not Chiang Kai-shek (or Czar Nicholas II), is the norm from which this new recalcitrant deviates. A former hero of the Revolution, Rubashov has grown progressively disillusioned with the regime that now represents it. The regime, he feels, has intensified the very ills which the Revolution was supposed to abolish, what with its one-man dictatorship and suppression of individual freedom; its forced labor camps, mass deportations, and executions; its sophisticated methods of mental and physical torture; its economic measures, so harsh that the average life-span has decreased; and its calculated sterilization of the masses. He finds even more intolerable the contradictions inherent in Party ideology itself, such as denying the existence of free will yet demanding of the individual a conscientious sense of duty, or presupposing "historical necessity" yet exhorting Communist man to make superhuman sacrifices to change the course of history.

Since he has always done the regime's bidding, Rubashov's disgust with the Party reflects a growing self-disgust. He has begun to be haunted by the friends he has betrayed or callously sacrificed, by the lies he has told and the crimes he has perpetrated, in order to carry out Party policy. It is not that he is just beginning to discover a "conscience." On the contrary, as a totally committed Communist, he has always been motivated by an extraordinary belief in his mission. Rubashov is actually a moral man who, like all underground men, has begun to question the foundation of his values—in his case, the regime. Whereas once he considered disobedience to the regime as the primary transgression, now he suspects that obedience to it may even be worse.

The basic cause of Rubashov's disenchantment is his rediscovery of something within him which, as a dedicated Party man, he has always rigorously suppressed. As he sits musing in prison, he becomes more and more cognizant of Rubashov-the-individual as distinguished from Rubashov-the-Communist. Always embarrassed by his own ego apart from the Party, he has till now denied its reality. There was no "I," but only

"We"; the "I" was something alien and impersonal, a "grammatical fiction."[7] Antedating his initiation as a Communist, this heretofore silent voice compels him to view himself and the Party from a forgotten code of humanistic ethics, challenging the primary Communist dictum that the end justifies the means, that expediency should have priority over human beings. Deliberately evoking Dostoevsky (even pacing the floor like Underground Man), Rubashov, who has begun to question the Chernyshevskian assumption that human destiny can be stated in a mathematical equation, now contends that possibly "twice two are not four when the mathematical units are human beings. . . ."

Contrary to Kyo, however, Rubashov is uneasy as a rebel. He is ambivalent. Like Underground Man visiting people whom he purports to hate, or Steppenwolf maintaining his ties with the bourgeoisie whom he lacerates, Rubashov would rather avoid a total break with the reigning Party. After all, since he has been a Communist most of his life, his new attitude of revolt must vie with the deeply entrenched thought patterns of the revolutionist. As Dostoevsky loved Christ but frowned on the Grand Inquisitor that represented him, so Rubashov affirms the Revolution (at least in the beginning of the novel), despite his disaffection from the regime which, he feels, has betrayed it. Because the Revolution is still a reality for him, he hesitates before he makes the final leap into underground.

When the regime demands that Rubashov confess to treason, he refuses, preferring instead to "die in silence." He knows the charges are absurd, believing that if he is guilty of anything, it is not plotting to overthrow the government but being too zealous in his service to it. Confessing to treason will only improve No. 1's image and brand Rubashov as a counterrevolutionary. Having devoted most of his life to the Revolution, he can hardly be expected to publicly dissociate himself from it now! Thus while he admits to being critical of the Party (though not to the point of taking action against it), he insists on his unqualified approval of the Revolution. To obtain a confession from him, the regime must first convince him that if he accepts the Revolution, he must also affirm the present regime—that there is, in fact, no other living representative of it.

Rubashov's ultimate capitulation is obtained through a series of "hearings" conducted by two successive interrogators, Ivanov and Gletkin.

---

[7] Arthur Koestler, *Darkness at Noon*, tr. Daphne Hardy, New York 1961. Subsequent quotations from *Darkness at Noon* are from this edition.

Although it is Gletkin to whom Rubashov makes the official confession, it is Ivanov who brings Rubashov around to the point where he is willing to confess in the first place. Ivanov breaks down Rubashov's resistance not through intimidation or torture, which he knows would be useless with the old Bolshevik, but through incisive dialectics. Ivanov, an old friend of Rubashov, knows how the latter thinks (he even secretly shares many of his views). By using many of Rubashov's past statements, he insidiously undermines Rubashov's current assumptions, eventually drawing from him the acknowledgment that what the regime wants is what he, Rubashov, has always wanted.

For every one of Rubashov's objections to the Party's tactics, Ivanov provides a justification which, since it answers to lingering convictions in Rubashov, has for the latter a ring of truth. The regime is oppressive? It has to be, answers Ivanov, because the "opposition" would like to overthrow it. Its economic policy is too austere? If it were less harsh, the nation's economy would collapse. No. 1 is ignoring the aims of the international Communist movement and only using it for his own purposes? There is currently a wave of "reaction" abroad that precludes revolution outside the country now and, in any case, world revolution is impossible until Communism is made secure at home.

But Ivanov directs his most impassioned barbs at Rubashov's dawning ethical qualms. Rubashov's moral objections to the regime are adduced from Christianity and bourgeois liberalism. But Ivanov declares that to the revolutionist, there is only one absolute: the Revolution. His basic assumption must be that

> ... a collective aim justifies all means, and not only allows, but demands, that the individual should be subordinated and sacrificed to the community—which may dispose of it as an experimentation rabbit or a sacrificial lamb.

Therefore, Rubashov's and Underground Man's aversion to applying the "laws of arithmetic" to individuals is ridiculous. ("That would mean a battalion commander may not sacrifice a patroling party to save the regiment.") To the revolutionary (and Ivanov clings tenaciously to the assumption that Rubashov is one), God and not Satan is the arch seducer:

> Sympathy, conscience, disgust, despair, repentance, and atonement are for us repellent debauchery.... The greatest temptation for the like of us is: to renounce violence, to repent, to make peace with

oneself. Most great revolutionaries fell before this temptation, from Spartacus to Danton and Dostoevsky; they are the classical form of betrayal to the cause. The temptations of God were always more dangerous for mankind than those of Satan. As long as chaos dominates the world God is an anachronism; and every compromise with one's own conscience is perfidy.

Ivanov's dialectic is not a blanket attack on Rubashov's tormented conscience, but only on what in it has been nurtured by Christian and humanistic standards. Indeed, his last rhetorical sally is precisely an appeal to conscience. Rubashov's scruples are, according to Ivanov, a base form of "moral cowardice" because he is shirking the consequence of the Revolution (incarnate in the present regime), in which he, Rubashov, played such a significant and historical role. His duty is to serve it, in devotion and humility, and not to be seeking a romantic, egoistical martyrdom.

This call to action is irresistable to Rubashov, especially when Ivanov promises him a light sentence and an opportunity to continue working for the Revolution. It is stronger, for the moment, than his inchoate bourgeois conscience, which Ivanov scornfully dismisses as "humanitarian scruples and other sentimentalities of that sort." Rubashov is convinced now that the only way he can be useful is to accommodate himself to the regime.

After his last talk with Ivanov, Rubashov begins to work out a justification of No. 1's methods. It is based on Marx's theory of the "logic of history," according to which we cannot evaluate present policies *in* the present. Actions can only be judged by their consequences, which are always by definition in the future. Therefore, only the future can tell, for example, whether No. 1 was correct in postponing world revolution or in suppressing individual freedom. At best, we can make informed guesses about present policy. So how can Rubashov be certain at this moment that No. 1 is pursuing a disastrous course?

> And what if, after all, No. 1 were right? If here, in dirt and blood and lies, after all and in spite of everything, the grandiose foundations of the future were being laid? Had not history always been an inhumane, unscrupulous builder, mixing its mortar of lies, blood, and mud?

With this dexterous rationalization, Rubashov is now ready to admit to minor acts of sedition, hoping he will be allowed to live and be useful to the Revolution (now the Party). But the regime, having eliminated his friend

Ivanov, now demands a total confession, including admission that Rubashov plotted to kill No. 1. Rubashov must die. But in addition, the regime asks him to stand trial and publicly declare that he is a contemptible counterrevolutionary and that the masses should reaffirm their loyalty to No. 1. At first he balks at this last assault on his personal dignity: to cooperate in such a "Punch and Judy show" would be the most absurd concession he has made thus far. Yet he agrees, because this last acquiescence would only be consistent with the position that Ivanov, and Rubashov's own tortuous logic, have thus far brought him to. In his own words, "Honor is: to serve without vanity, and unto the last consequence."

At the trial that ensues, Rubashov discharges his last role consummately. The former hero of the Revolution ensures his lasting infamy with the declaration:

> There is nothing for which one could die, if one died without having repented and unreconciled with the Party and the Movement. Therefore, on the threshold of my last hour, I bend my knees to the country, to the masses and to the whole people. The political masquerade, the mummery of discussions and conspiracy are over. We were politically dead long before the Citizen Prosecutor demanded our heads.

With this (his execution is anticlimactic), Rubashov pays his last due to the Party. It can demand no more of him.

Between his trial and execution, however, Rubashov begins to settle other accounts. Till now, under the unceasing pressure of the interrogations, his chief preoccupation has been with his role as a Communist. Now, having disposed of that question and knowing he has only a few hours to live, he discovers that he is still profoundly dissatisfied. Why, indeed, is he dying? The temporarily suppressed "grammatical fiction," that subjective "I" which defines Rubashov as an entity distinct from the Party, springs into consciousness again; and now, cognizant of its imminent extinction, it compels Rubashov to view critically not only the Party but also the Revolution itself, which he has already identified with the Party. In the privacy of his cell, Rubashov admits for the first time what he could never have voiced at the trial, that the Revolution has failed. With this admission, he finally and unequivocally declares himself an underground man.

With the emergence of the repressed "I," more peremptory now than it ever was, Rubashov is repelled by the moral and spiritual sterility of the Communist state. The fundamental moral fallacy, in the name of which he has sacrified others and is now sacrificing himself, is the precept that the end justifies the means:

> It was this sentence which had killed the great fraternity of the Revolution and made them all run amuck. What had he once written in his diary? "We have thrown overboard all conventions; our sole guiding principle is that of consequent logic; we are sailing without ethical ballast."

Even if Communism were to realize its highest aims, man would still be moving about in Chernyshevsky's empty Crystal Palace. Echoing Underground Man's scorn for a purely amoral and materialistic utopia (the allusion is unmistakable), Rubashov is dubious of the Communist "palace":

> But what did it look like inside? No, one cannot build paradise with concrete. The bastion would be preserved, but it no longer had a message or an example to give the world. No. 1's regime had besmirched the ideal of the Social State even as some medieval popes had besmirched the ideal of a Christian Empire. The flag of the Revolution was at half-mast.

In challenging the first principles of Communism (Underground Man's *brick wall*), Rubashov has left constrictive political theory for the unfamiliar realm of metaphysics. Suddenly, he becomes conscious of the infinite—of the sky, the night, the elemental universe around him—and of his uncertain relation to it. Like Koestler himself sitting in a Spanish prison, he is overwhelmed by this "oceanic sense." It is not new to him, but he has always scoffed at it, just as he has always denied his individual ego: it was always "*petit-bourgeois* mysticism, refuge in the ivory tower." But now he begins to ask, not what is a Communist, but what is man, and what is his ultimate destiny beyond Communism or any other ideology? Rubashov is appalled at his ignorance of these fundamental metaphysical questions. Here (he recognizes in his final moments) is the "real source of his guilt." But this acknowledgment comes too late—he can hardly be expected to resolve in a few minutes what, say, Kafka and Dostoevsky's Underground Man pondered throughout their adult lives.

Some readers may be disturbed by the last twenty pages of *Darkness at Noon,* in which Rubashov gives free vent to these metaphysical reflections, for they follow a more thorough and dramatic portrayal of his loyalties as a Communist. Nonetheless, Koestler takes great pains to present Rubashov as a man in conflict, whose doubts are apparent from the outset. Rubashov's criticism of Communism in the conclusion contradicts his actions immediately preceding it because he never successfully resolves his conflict. He still believes in the ends of Communism: it is only for the means that he now feels revulsion. What he is groping for, moments before he dies, is some distant and perhaps impossible synthesis of religion and Communism (what Koestler will later call the "yogi" and the "commissar"):

> Perhaps later, much later, the new movement would arise—with new flags, a new spirit knowing of both: of economic fatality *and* the "oceanic sense."

Thus Rubashov dreams of a utopia more ambitious than either Chernyshevsky's or Dostoevsky's, combining the material prosperity of the one with the spirituality of the other. Rubashov, the once atheistic, rationalistic, "scientific" Bolshevik, dies grasping for the Promised Land. But he knows, as did Kafka and Dostoevsky before him, that the vineyards of plenty can only be rooted in spiritual soil, from which the Revolution has hopelessly strayed:

> Did there really exist any such goal for this wandering mankind? That was a question to which he would have liked an answer before it was too late. Moses had not been allowed to enter the land of promise either. But he had been allowed to see it, from the top of the mountain, spread at his feet.... He, Nicolas Salmanovitch Rubashov, had not been taken to the top of a mountain; and wherever his eye looked, he saw nothing but desert and the darkness of night.

Contrary to the Communist Kyo, whose death gives meaning to his life, Comrade Rubashov dies doubting everything he has done for the Party in the past forty years. He does conceive a substitute ideal for dialectical materialism. But it is fuzzy, and in all probability it is unobtainable. In any event, death spares him the responsibility of testing it against the harsh light of reality. He is therefore caught, with Sartre's Existentialist, between a nonexistent future and a dead past, even possibly being in "bad faith" because of his dubious attitude toward that past. And were he allowed to live longer, he would probably come to resemble more and more those other underground men: Kafka, Jean Baptiste, the early Steppenwolf, and Dostoevsky's original anti-hero. For then he would be doomed to live in a society which daily became more abhorent to him and challenged his tenuous idealism. The execution of this useless old underground man is deliberately stripped of pomp and beauty (instead of dying before a firing squad in an open courtyard, he dies from two dull bullets pumped into the back of his head by a single executioner in a subterranean corridor of the prison). Yet, it is a merciful end.

CONCLUSION

In the seven novels we have surveyed after *Notes from Underground,* underground man has expressed himself in a variety of ways. Each novel stresses different reasons why men go underground, and with the possible exception of Kafka, each author eventually offers some form of affirmation (God, revolt, art) which is totally lacking in Dostoevsky's novel (although it is to be found in his subsequent works). Underground man is only a model, of which Dostoevsky's protagonist is the quintessential example. Subsequent underground men differ from him according to the specific historical conditions that produce them and the personal predilections of their creators. Nonetheless, all of these characters, along with the tortured Kafka and Genet, experience anguish, estrangement, heightened consciousness turning in upon itself, and impotent rage at being reduced to two times two equals four. And to that extent they retain their essential kinship with Dostoevsky's Underground Man.